PLUSH

PLUSH

SELECTED POEMS
OF
SKY GILBERT
COURTNAY McFARLANE
JEFFERY CONWAY
R.M. VAUGHAN
&
DAVID TRINIDAD

Edited by Lynn Crosbie & Michael Holmes

COACH
HOUSE

For Peter McGehee

He is a portion of the loveliness
Which once he made more lovely ...

Coach House Press, Toronto
© The contributors, 1995. All rights reserved.

FIRST EDITION
1 3 5 7 9 8 6 4 2
Printed in Canada

Published with the assistance of the Canada Council, the Department of Canadian Heritage, the
Ontario Arts Council and the Ontario Publishing Centre.
R.M. Vaughan thanks the Canada Council, the Ontario Arts Council and the New Brunswick
Ministry of Culture.

Editor for the Press: Lynn Crosbie
Text Design: Nathalie Butterfield

Canadian Cataloguing in Publication Data
Main entry under title:

Plush
ISBN 0-88910-481-6

1. Gay men — Poetry.
2. Gays' writings, Canadian (English).*
3. Gays' writings, American.
4. Canadian poetry (English) — 20th century.*
5. American poetry — 20th century.
I. Crosbie, Lynn, 1963–
II. Holmes, Michael, 1966–
PS8287.H65P58 1995   C811'.5408'0353   C95-931949-2
PR9195.85.H65P58 1995

CONTENTS

INTRODUCTION

On the way, a boy made an ambiguous gesture in my direction. "Was he spitting at me?" I said recalling the political situation. "No," said Nigel, "he was blowing you a kiss." I'm glad things have returned to normal.
—Joe Orton, June 1967

When we began assembling this anthology the title presented itself, ready to wear. Plush fabric had begun to appear everywhere, resplendent—in bright pinks and neon greens—on the heads and shoulders of everyone from teenage boys to slap-up, stylish men. Plush, that softer than velvet, lavish material, best gestured to the work of the five writers we wanted to include in this collection. The poems of Jeffery Conway, Sky Gilbert, Courtnay McFarlane, David Trinidad and R.M. Vaughan are smart, stylish and striking. Cut from the same vivid cloth, each writer is an original. And although *there can never be enough sparkles*, PLUSH presents five of the most stellar gay poets working in North America today.

We first encountered each of these writers at readings. As poets, we soon learned never to read after Gilbert or Vaughan: their tumultuous performances are impossible acts to follow. Similarly, Conway and McFarlane are as mesmerizing as snake-charmers, while Trinidad's deadpan delivery belies every poetic revolution he stages.

Reading their work only served to amplify our admiration—their poems are skillfully crafted, thoughtful, intricate and gorgeous studies of the intersection of the personal and political, and their explorations of form and genre incorporate experience, influence and cultural reference to create voices that are distinctive, playful and penetrating. Each of these writers produces inspirational and integral poetry, from bold invocations of pop iconography and provocative meditations upon the complexities of love and desire to subtle revisions of how issues of gender, race, class and sex are perceived. Together, their words—grounded emphatically in gay experience—resonate as a testimony to "the hope that concerns us all", to paraphrase Nicole Brossard.

Initially, we conceived this anthology as a means of expressing and celebrating our deep affinity for the love, anger, passion and determination that these writers evoke. In the process of editing PLUSH, our conviction grew that the poems—words and work all to often neglected by the mainstream—spoke both to one another and to a much wider audience than any notion of an anthology of gay poets could possibly suggest. Our role as editors became remarkably clear: we merely had to (like the pages in a passion play) prompt the action, the drama that the poets themselves had already set in motion.

The five poets who compose the cast of PLUSH offer everything but tedium: *there's only chemistry ... and power.*

LYNN CROSBIE AND MICHAEL HOLMES
SEPTEMBER 1995

SKY GILBERT

THE ISLAND OF LOST TEARS

Haven't you heard the latest news about AIDS?
You can get it from tears
O yes
You mustn't let anyone cry on you or
cry near you, in fact it's a very good idea not to let anyone cry in the same
room as you
We have received notice that at the moment authorities are considering
taking all the weepers (all the wettest people in the world)—shipping them
off, and putting them on a small island off Southern England where they
can all weep on each other to their heart's content and it rains there all the
time anyway so they won't know the difference
And all those great movies
the tearjerkers:
The Heiress, Now Voyager, Madame X, Love Is a Many Splendored Thing,
The Rainmaker, The Rains of Ranchipur and even for you really sappy
ones, parts of The Music Man
will no longer be allowed on TV
And if you know someone who's a sentimental type you'd better warn them,
you'd better have a heart to heart or safer yet, a mind to mind and say
"In the past you were wont to get emotional at the slightest provocation.
Though there's nothing really wrong with being emotional—everyone, in
the past, got emotional from time to time—now, because of what we know
about tears, it's better that you try to control yourself and not get into
situations where you might be moved. You know ... one thing leads to
another and just taking casual notice of a impoverished beggar woman or
watching a sunset for an extended length of time, for many, could lead to
such minor yet dangerous feelings as sadness, love, pity, affection, and
from these it is but a short step to the dreaded tears. For some even the
old fashioned notion of warmth will become a thing of the past. Certainly
old habits die hard, many will be unwilling to give up their emotional lives.
But the danger to human health is too great. Do yourself a favour. Stop
feeling deeply. Your partner, your lover, your husband wife or significant
other will thank you for your consideration in repressing your deepest most
profound emotions."

But me
I will go
To the Island of Lost Tears
No boat will take you there
No plane will fly you there
You must find your own way
Some swim, some walk on the water
Some claim they fly there
And as you approach
you can hear the faint sounds of sobbing
and you see nothing
but a lush greenery shrouded in mist
And when you reach the shore
they rush to you
and hold you
in their strong arms
arms made so much stronger warmer by being caressed with tears
And they take you to their
wet little houses
and sit you down by their
wet little fires
and they say to you
"Cry
my sweet boy
my inscrutable girl
cry until you have no more tears
until the very well that is your sadness and your joy is dry
and when you think that you can cry no more
you find that you can cry still!"
No one dies there
in the Island of Lost Tears
they simply fade into the mist
But late at night through the trees
(they have none but weeping willows)
the voices whisper the forbidden words
"Weep ... cry ... feel ... let yourself go!"
These are the ghosts of those who dared
to cry when all others had forgotten how, and they will not be silenced

THE RAINS OF RANCHIPUR

Why can't I
be like the woman on the Camay commercial
She gets a phone message from this really
sexy guy when she gets home from her classy job
and takes off her hat ... "Sorry I missed you, I'll call later"
And then she decides to take a bath
with Camay
And she's all covered with bubbles
and she just smiles
and sinks down lower into those bubbles
what is she smiling about?
Why doesn't she answer the phone?
Me, I'm much more like
Myrna Loy in
When The Rains Came
And there's a plague in Ranchipur
and she looks at Tyrone Power
who is wearing a surgical mask right now
because he's a surgeon
even though he's destined to be a prince and
will have to give her up
and she gazes at him

and he asks
"Why did you decide to work here, as a nurse
when you could still be a superficial
promiscuous witty party girl in long shimmering dresses?"
And she lowers her surgical mask
and you just know she wants to say
"Because I love you
I'll always love you, Tyrone Power who will
have to become prince someday and
give me up!"
And he kisses her
and for a moment they forget to disinfect
It's true
you're not a surgeon prince
and I don't have eyes like Myrna Loy
You're a maintenance technician
and you forgot to phone me on Saturday Night
So why
when you phone me today
don't I just lower myself into my bubble bath and smile?
Because
even if the maharani of Ranchipur ordered me to get on
an airplane and become a superficial party girl again
I'll always remember
the way you surrender
when I press you into the pillow
and I kiss you

ON FAME

It was the Halloween when Ernie said
"That year we lived in the same house
you were a great influence on me"
And the woman outside the theatre yelled
"You are a God!" as I lurched towards Yonge Street
in my high heels
Richard was being vicious
or Eddie was being sensitive
It's hard for me to be sure
Bruno said "I've never seen you looking so beautiful"
Onstage I sang a song
Everyone clapped and seemed to think I was talented
It seems to matter little
As the thunder of the applause dies down
That James does not succeed in getting an erection
and pulls his limp dick out of my waiting ass
Holding the soggy condom he inquires
"Where should I put this?"
"Why, on the plush velvet cushion" I say
Being the queen that I am
It's not that I want to be loved by one particular person or anything
That would be asking too much
It's kind of this trade you make
The respect of many
For the passion of one
And there might not have been a velvet cushion
when the sad and sorry fucking was done

ASSFUCKING AND JUNE ALLYSON

(I can't believe I got them both in one poem)
You know what it's like when you start to argue with them
I mean really argue
And they're twenty one years old (just turned)
and then you start to fall in "like"?
It's that night when you first think
I'm going to remember this night and I'm going to look back on it
and I'm going to think about how he got so gleefully energetically
angry
And then the fight
And this night the fight was about assfucking without a condom
theoretical—no really—
not that we would I mean ... really engage in (gosh!)
But he's twenty one years old and he only came out three years ago
and he doesn't really understand what it feels like
or what makes it so wonderful
And I realize it's as important
as remembering June Allyson's voice
to describe to him what it was like
So just pretend you're twenty one years old
and you have incredibly blonde hair
and you've never ever heard June Allyson speak (except on those
golden age diaper commercials which don't really count!)
You don't even know who she is

and so I have to somehow describe how
June Allyson's voice sort of came from down there
sort of deep and very felt
but it was sweet
and harsh
and when you needed it most
it was always there
And sometimes you hated it
sometimes it got on your nerves
but then when you got down to it
there was nothing quite like June Allyson's voice
And that's what it was like to fuck somebody in the ass without a
condom
And you're twenty one years old
and you'll get mad at me for writing this poem
and you'll probably want to scratch my back with your incredibly
long nails
but that's alright
because someday in 1999 when they've found a cure for AIDS
I'll actually shove my dick up your ass without a condom
and you'll open your mouth, meaning to say
"What the hell do you think you're—"
and instead
you'll end up talking like June Allyson
which is, as I said
sometimes painful
but more often than not, incredibly, incredibly wonderful

WHY YOU DON'T HAVE TO BE GAY TO
UNDERSTAND THE SAGRADA FAMILIA BUT IT HELPS

I remember when friend many years ago showed me a picture of it
of the Sagrada Familia
Gaudi's famous masterpiece
a church
I was amazed.
But I was a heterosexual then so I didn't really understand.
You see the church itself was never really finished but there is a façade and
an empty shell behind (gay aspect #1)
Though a spiritual building the edifice is firmly grounded in mud in cave
dwellings and the very top of the spires are decorated with multicoloured
stars (gay aspect #2; see Oscar Wilde—"We are all in the gutter but some
of us are looking at the stars.")
But what one feels most of all gazing at the Sagrada Familia is reaching,
reaching higher still and inevitably falling and one thinks of Jeannie Beker
on Fashion Television doing a Gaudi program—
"Was he drunk?" she asks—
an in-depth question
Yes Gaudi was drunk and so am I on the Catalan boy I met last night bright
eyes 22 hair on his lovely ass (thank God for his hairy legs, they made him
wonder at my hairless ones) and we made feverish love in my hot little room
and my hand up his ass to the knuckles and he a very charming red flushed
boy colour
And after he tells me about Catalonia, his country, and mountain building—
and I don't understand. And he says "We like to build mountains here in
Catalonia," and I still don't understand and he says "People get together and
climb on top of each other and make mountains—the smallest at the top—
we will be doing it at the Olympics" and I ask him—"Why do you do this
in Catalonia, make mountains?" and he laughs and says—"We just do."
We just do.
And you Gaudi make this thing this structure this Sagrada Familia and like
all Christian artists you made a minor mistake it's supposed to be a monu-
ment of God to the spirit of the Holy Ghost but no it is not that at all it is a
monument to the spirit of man Yes we can make mountains we can shape the
mud into stars and yes oh yes
My Catalan boy I think I understand now why you do it
why you make mountains ...

SEVEN SILLINESSES ABOUT OPERA
THAT REMIND ME OF YOU

1. Meeting Again and Starting Up as if Nothing Happened

I mean I don't remember why I said goodbye to you
Yes I do you were too young I guess
And we didn't seem to have anything to say to each other
And I was very foolhardy and imagined my back wouldn't go
    into spasm for three months after I said goodbye to you
But it did
And now that I've invited you out to dinner
The possibility that we might pick up where we left off
is as silly and romantic as opera
it boggles the mind

2. Laughing to Music

Ha ha ha
They go
To the music, in time
They aren't really laughing are they
They are frivolous prostitutes who speak no dirty words
But have pretty dresses and flowers in their hair
And laugh in time to the music
Ha ha ha
That reminds me of you

3. That Moment When the Melody

That moment when the melody just disappears fades away and
    they seem to be arguing with their voices, mumbling
It's like the collective unconscious or something
They seem to have forgotten what they are singing
But it comes back
Perhaps that's what happened to us
We forgot what we were singing for a moment
The memory of the melody just disappeared
Now it's floating back
It's always there you see
It just depends on whether or not our ears are cocked
So to speak
To hear it

4. When They Sing "L'amour L'amour"

Like my old friend Christopher used to say
"Oh ... they're just going on about love.."
And they do for quite a bit. At least 32 bars.
It's as if love were important and not just this construct that we got
    from our parents, something to kill time with

5. He Sits Down at the Piano

He sits down at the piano and plays a tune and
suddenly everyone can sing it, perfectly in key and harmonizing
and everyone knows the words but the words are particularly apt
to their own particular lives and situations.
You still like to get fucked up the bum, don't you?
For hours?

Only now I know I'll have to use a condom (and pull out too,
    because I do truly love you)
And you still moan the way you did?
And squirm?
And are you still just as embarrassed about having orgasms?
I don't think so.
But that's okay.

6. They Meet at a Café

They meet at a café or party or something and fall in love
immediately even though they have nothing in common and her
murderous husband is standing over there in the corner singing
    and he has a knife
I can't imagine what we had in common
Looking back on it now
Except that you liked to watch TV and gossip
Two of my favorite things
And you were unpretentious
And your hair was so curly
And you used to be a swimmer and your body
But I digress

7. The Heroine Is Always Fat

Always has been always will be but somehow the hero who is a
    handsome young poet or painter or revolutionary does not notice
that he can't get his arms around her
In my mind (always being the fat boy)
You might never get your arms around me
But I imagine your beautiful face
Yearning stretching trying
Your arms reaching
And you not noticing
Really not noticing
That it takes any effort at all

REFLECTIONS ON JUDY

for Nick

Of course I was very stoned and there were lots of campy guys and cruising guys standing
    around but

There she was

(end of Mrs. Dalloway, literary reference, some sort of image of feminine ascendancy meaning
    everything feminine or the essence of of of)

Too many sparkles (can there ever be too many sparkles?)

And she knows HOW to wear that dress

(but daahhhhrling)

How many drugs is she on?

Which ones?

Yes long legs, but the dress is too tight

When she sits down we feel for her tummy

And the hair, a maniacal pageboy

And from certain angles she's in Meet Me In St. Louis again

And Liza's only a baby

From other angles she's a hundred years old and Liza is stiff competition

And why do we care?

Why do we care about this very wrecked lady, who is almost as wrecked as we are?

Oh there she goes again

She's gone into some sort of frenzy, arms all akimbo

Is it because she's just like every desperate drunken horny woman you've ever met at a party,
    only she has talent (lots of)?

What do she and Mick Jagger have in common?

Only we don't stand in a bar watching Mick Jagger on video and feel sort of sad and mushy
    and a little bit guilty, do we?

And people might call us sadistic for wondering how long she can really stand up

There she goes again her arms flailing around what do arms mean? Reaching? I want? Give
    me ... I'm dying, give me

And the applause the audience applause how melodramatic the applause that killed her

Too melodramatic I'm staggering into my drink it's late I'm thinking of you and an alley and
you probably knew I'd get into an alley it's all a pretense writing a poem about Judy Garland
it's really a poem about you and what I wonder is do you remember? You probably remember
Do you think someone heard us? Does it matter? Were we being silly? Are you actually an evil
manipulator? Can you actually believe I find you INTERESTING? And dramatic? Has anyone
ever written a poem for you before? This poem has gone on too long

I should get back to Judy Garland

Here I am standing in a bar watching a little faggot dance under a video of Judy Garland

He is very stoned

So am I

I'm think about you

and Judy Garland

Interesting combination

AN ISOLATED HOMOSEXUAL INDECENCY

It was an isolated incident like no other
a case of homosexual love
unnoticed by the press
there was no murder, killing
no suicide
there were no notes, feathers, declamatory gestures, no makeup, couriers or
discursive worriers, no falling tones, singing queens, dying stars, lies,
rejection, beer smelling, swilling or spilling, there were no shoddy hot toddies
or party girls pressed into minutiae, pressured for an opinion, dismissed
dismayed, on display, depressed and desiring, expiring in boas
or quotas
There was just me on the couch,
okay, I was not not feeling very well
and you had just found the perfect apartment
and you came running into the room
but I was on the phone of course
gossiping with Ann
and petting the cat
and you were so filled with joy
and you looked so damn beautiful
and your skin was so white
and your fingers were so long
as they grazed your skin
moving that stray strand of hair off your young, smiling face
that I just had to grab you
and come all over you
and then lie there late and exhausted
in the last gasp of the afternoon sun.
You didn't seem to mind.
If it had been printed in the papers
I would have been poised by the window, at midnight

(a creature of the dark)
in a platinum dress
a heated sheath
burning my tender skin
the gun would be smoking
you would be lying
on the floor
nasty fecal stains would have been
found
on your underwear
and discussed by the police
ad nauseum.
But of course, the truth is as boring and paltry as this:
I came all over you one afternoon
because I was happy about you and your new apartment.
Is it we who distort our reality, or "they"
Either way,
it's no wonder we can't seem to get
same sex spousal
benefits
(platinum dresses, your gorgeous tresses, can't seem to find, get you out of my
mind, you on the bed, confusion in my head, transpire, perspire, the glare,
heat, hair, I dare you to care—it's me, no it's you, no it's all of us too, we
confess, we digress it's all such a mess, but we must have the fuss, it's so very
us, the way we are, pinned on a star, believe it or not, it's got to be hot, or
else if it's not, life's such a bore, we most fear a snore, see you later queen!
or else in a dream—au revoir, mon petit chou, my little cabbage,
coming all over you was fun,
love,
me)

LIGHTER THAN AIR

When people ask me what I see in younger men I always think of walking
past Christ Church in Montreal before it was the mall
"Under construction" people used to stop and stare
They dug out the basement of the church and it seemed suspended it seemed
to be flying the buttresses like wings the cool dry underbelly brightly lit by work
lights—what happens underneath the church? What goes on? What supports
it? What are those men doing underneath that church?
Those were the days when Christ Church Montreal floated above St.
Catherine's Street and the passersby stopped to stare, wondering why it was
suddenly lighter than air
Recently I walked by Christ Church
The construction is completed
The cool bright underbelly has been encased in concrete
No one really looks at the new church now
"It's an architectural marvel" they say, "a church with a mall underneath" and
walk away without blinking
And I think of Dennis, 22, clear bright eyes, a shock of hair that reaches down
to his chin "I have to get it cut" and when I painted a picture for him it was
"the best present I ever got" and Dennis is the best present I ever got because
he is perched absolutely expectant, only the best ahead, absolutely romantic
and I've never seen his large full cock when it wasn't erect
It is, I suppose callous of me to want Dennis now instead of 20 years from
now when people will walk by him without blinking and when his yearning
will be encased in concrete
I want my men under construction, lighter than air and I can still wonder what
holds them up, with their cocks arched like flying buttresses and their
eyelashes fluttering like wings

ONCE WHEN I WAS IN A PLAY

Once when I was in a play I was dead
(Hamlet killed me; I, Claudius)
and it was a very long play
and I was very tired
And they picked me up and placed me in a white canvas bag
and carried me off into a secluded backstage area
And what would always happen was
Sean, a young man, would open the bag
and there I would be, dead
lying on the floor in the canvas bag
And there would be Sean, tall dark curly haired with those thick
unwholesome lips, Sean with the conceited chest hair and the cocky
grin and buttocks that I had never seen but caught a glimpse of (one
day, when we tied him up, did I tell you about that? no? well me and
some of the girls—the adolescents in the company—tied up Sean one
day when we had nothing else to do and then we tortured him, yes we
did, we poured cold water on his nipples and made him cry pitifully
and sensuously and boyishly and he writhed and writhed just so that
we could look at his body better and I whipped him with wet shoelaces
and things and for an hour or two it was as if we were in love Sean
and I except that he was simply tied to this old couch and me and a
bunch of adolescent girls were just having some afternoon fun)
and when I woke up, dead, every night, at the end of Hamlet,
there was Sean
standing above me
with that silly-so-pleased-with-himself-smile
(Sean was always wanting to take his clothes off, and why not? his
    body was so pretty)
And so that's what it's like, I thought,
when you're gay, and dead
A pretty boy like Sean
unwraps you
and you smile at him
and you stand up
"Pretty long play eh?" says Sean
and he slaps you on the back jovially with his big Irishslashltalian hand
and then it's off to heaven
In case you were wondering what happens to gay guys when they
    die, that's it
I found out because of
once when I was in a play

ANGELS

1. **Very popular right now.**
   According to Time Magazine
   we are seeing a resurgence of angels.
   Who can account for the unprecedented popularity
   of these winged cherubs?
   Could it be a return to spiritual values?
   Red faced,
   Ruddy,
   Like real children
   Except that their penises and clits have been brutally
   Chopped off
   By painters and sculptors offended by such plush, redundant,
   resplendent appendages.
   Angels—
   soft, cuddly, sweet, divine, laughing, gurgling, cooing, waxing waning, never
   complaining, pink, dimpled, chubby, draped in white never see the dark of night,
   peering over a cloud at break of day, the gates of heaven,
   ah for the imagined innocence of a prepubescent smile
   ah, for a smile worth violating

2. I like angels

Also.
I like to see them going at it.
You know.
I like to see angels fucking.
They don't look so goddamn cherubic then.
Dirty grimy bloodstained angels,
smelling of shit and semen
(does semen smell?)
they sniff each other's assholes
assholes redolent and hairy
oops a cling-on!
angels in dirty underwear
an angel with a hardon
when pink turns purple
dimpled cheeks strain
with desire
"Jesus Christ"
They cry,
these little dappled whores
fucking on a cloud is kinda
like a waterbed
and all that water
kinda makes a girl wanna piss
open your mouth honey
this angel is gonna drop a load on you.
What kind of load?
Don't know
Let me open up. See what comes out.
Ughghg.

3. There I am, having a hot chocolate,

at the Second Cup

not even feeling attractive.

He sits down.

Hi.

Very blonde from Belleville just broke up with his lover who he still lives with but he's

not rushing into anything, says he.

Meanwhile, I have barely had time to say hello.

No, let's not rush into anything, angel, I think.

"I can't,

Because of my condition," he says.

What condition?

I ask.

"I'm HIV positive," he says.

Ah.

Doe eyes

brown eyes, my little HIV positive angel

I look down

ahh, yes

strangely enough

you do have a penis

let me touch it

ahh

Let's see what comes out

SOME INCIDENTS THAT HAPPENED ON MY VACATION

1. IN NEW YORK CITY at the Universal Restaurant with all the upscale fags drinking and being trendy and it was someone's birthday and they put on an old disco song and pulled out a cake and a cute waiter put on a hat and lip-synched and there on a cold night in February amidst all the AIDS deaths and suffering and my friend a young writer who wanted my opinion on his play so I took advantage of him and his social set for one night turned and said to me "It doesn't get gayer than this, does it?"
True.
But actually it does really because later I went to this sleazy little fuck club called PRISM on 9th Avenue—you just get out of the cab, you don't look around—and found myself after 8 beers with my ass in the air and a huge black stud slapping it shoving either under my nose yelling "TAKE THAT ON YOUR BIG WHITE BUBBLE BUTT!" while several fags watched
Oh Mark, I beg to differ but it did get gayer than that.
It did.
So after being suitably chastised for being in possession of a big white bubble butt, it was time to go visit my father.

2. IN CONNECTICUT things were quieter. I love my dad but he watches TV a lot. And he tried so hard he'd been reading up about theatre and he asked me questions. But basically we watched a lot of TV. And even though there's four TV's, one in the living room one in the bedroom, one in the den and one in the DINING ROOM, believe it or not, the DINING ROOM, still, we had TV wars—I just could not watch tennis or golf. So there was me in the living room watching TO HAVE AND TO HAVE NOT—it's not really a very good movie except for "PUT YOUR LIPS TOGETHER AND BLOW"—did Hemingway write that line? I doubt it—anyway, Dad, Stepmother, and Stepgrandmother are huddled in the den watching tennis. Oh I felt so guilty! And horny. So at one o'clock in the morning when all were long asleep I locked myself in the downstairs john and jerked off on the toilet. Which was okay, cleaned up

frantically and flushed, then the next day I took a shit in the same toilet and of course it wouldn't flush. Oh no. Stopped up and four or five big light brown turds floating around in it, impervious to my anxiety. An impervious turd, what an oxymoron. Anyway, I nonchalantly strolled to the living room to watch TV and sneaked back ten minutes later to try again but no luck no flush, ambled innocently back to watch TV suddenly my stepmother emerges from the john "The toilets plugged up!" Well you've never seen such excitement, she and my father run to the toilet to examine my turds. "I did it," I confess. I wouldn't want them to think that those horrible shits belonged to Granny, she gets in enough trouble for being senile and fucking up her knitting, poor old gal. "Sky," says my stepmother, who is a registered nurse, "why didn't you tell us?" Well, this is my big moment, I think, I can be honest. Bare my soul. "I didn't tell you," I say, "because I was embarrassed." "Oh," says my stepmother, sizing me up in that condescending fraught with deep not so hidden hatred Nurse Ratched sort of way that drives me insane, "why would you be embarrassed?" because of course she is a nurse and is just so goddamned comfortable with bodily functions. Hah! I think Hah! If you knew I'd jerked off on the same toilet last night you'd have a fucking heart attack. You love looking at my shit, but one look at my cum and you'd be screaming bloody murder, like somebody knifed you. Anyway, Dad unplugged the toilet, things calmed down and it was time to watch the 6 o'clock news.

3. IN KEY WEST Last night I went to Aunt Lolly's Corner Grocery Store to buy some beer. And Aunt Lolly asked me for ID. I couldn't believe it! I was so happy! "I'm thirty-nine years old Aunt Lolly!" I beamed. "Well," she said, "tell me your birthdate." I did. She handed me the beer. "Can't be too careful," observed Aunt Lolly. "We get a lot of spring-breakers in here!" Oh! Aunt Lolly—you made an old fag so happy!

4. IN KEY WEST So he was young blonde and sadistic as my postcard said and he made me think why oh why are people LIKE that. Certainly a little healthy sadism at the right time is okay but I picked him up at the Number One Saloon, he a southern boy cute accent, 29 yes, but eternally boyish Greg, sex is always good with a slender boy, even when it's bad, only problem he wanted desperately to fuck me without a condom. BUZZ warning signal, I should realize for future reference that in 1992 this is psychotic behaviour. Anyway needless to say I didn't let him, but fisted him instead. We talked he seemed

actually charming but I am easily charmed by those of his ilk. Gave him my address in Key West, he said he'd drop by next day. Next day I woke early thinking of him, gussied myself up, didn't floss, waited, then noticed that he had left my address on the table. Oh well. Went to the beach, who should be there but him. We chat. Rub oil on each other, make the other fags on the beach talk. Next, lunch he pays he proves to be a spoiled rich kid originally from Atlanta, he abuses the waitress in a charming way he obviously hates women and he's reminding me of my ex boyfriend, pretty enough to get away with murder. I invite him back to my place Jeffrey Dahmer is on Geraldo oddly enough we start making love while watching Geraldo's tasteless tabloid interview with Dahmer's last almost victim we make jokes about it all, move to the bedroom. Sex is enjoyable but he keeps pushing his fingers up my butt, not in a nice way, not even in a nice fisting way, I mean it starts out nice and as soon as it feels good he starts hurting me, and I realize as he gazes into my eyes that he's enjoying this, enjoying my very real discomfort. I am not. Sex over he gets dressed will I see you tonight and he's gazing at me in that way someone does when they're falling for you. Gosh this is flattering but frightening, I say we can start boozing together at 10:30 at the 801 he agrees. Oh God the way he looks at me scares me half to death—you can't adore me yet you don't know me—we meet later he seems a tiny bit drunk not much, is gazing at me too much after two vodkas he suddenly is staggering falling asleep at least semi-permanently on the barstool, he says "You're a really hot man, you know?" again I'm very flattered but so sad he had to get this polluted just to say it. Then he punches me. Not hard but as he drifts into oblivion he gazes at me dreamily and punches my chest my thigh I realize that it is his attraction to me this big guy that he can't handle, desires me greatly but definitely wants to hurt me how sad how sad I leave him asleep on the barstool I hope he's okay.

5. IN KEY WEST I realize I am aurtistic, that's a combination of artistic and autistic. What do I mean by this—well autism is described by ex-autistics as being a state where everything hurts, every human contact, a caress becomes a blow a punch, the scrape of sandpaper on skin love equals dermabrasion and with me it's when people love me when I try to love them I am so overwhelmed by all their needs tortured trying to fulfill them please them I get afraid run from the intimacy so I can only relate to those who need nothing want nothing no guilt no pressure ultimately no relationship I must work on this problem or perhaps I can't oh well at least I wrote all this down that's the artistic part.

6. IN KEY WEST I write a poem:

THE NIGHT I DREAMED RICKY RICARDO WAS MY FATHER

Well it's possible.
I mean time-wise and all.
Well when Lucy was pregnant and in the hospital on TV so was my mother.
I was born about one month before Little Ricky.
And I was early.
And I'm very dark and musically talented but a bit wacky and I had a drum
set which I never played when I was kid.
So like it's possible really maybe he was and in my dream I'm sitting looking
at him at Ricky Ricardo senior and he's sitting in one of those grand southern
cane backed chairs and he's wearing a tux but the tie is casually off to the
side and he's so fucking attractive and we're chatting and I can't believe it
he is my father!
And suddenly my whole life has changed because my dad isn't this lovable
balding fat sexless old man
He's young and horny with bright dark eyes
And of course I understand how I got like this how I got this permanently
hard dick this libido from hell it's from Dad from Ricky and it all make sense
It's nice to have a reason for being the way you are
And having a dad that understands you know?
Now I just have to deal with the fact that Lucy is my mother.

COURTNAY McFARLANE

RUMINATIONS

for Douglas

O n e

In these days of Proud Lives
posthumous portraits
measuring/1"x 3/4"
a name/two dates
stamped on inky newsprint
a life is remembered
only in (it's)
passing

I am reminded
of men who go/unrecalled
lives in/visible duppy men:
who lived in compartment & died
accompanied only/by the sound
of their own breathing

Of spaces
where HIV is mere fodder
for gossip & kee/keeing
like details of workouts/dicksize
Dreaded as thoughts of our (friend's)
    deaths
whispered in mind/not spoken

We moved
around the circle
Black/proud & mouth
but did not say
gay

T w o

I marched up Yonge St.
carried banners on Pride Day
years before/I told my mother
I was gay

Pre/occupied
in flight from familial spaces
frowsy with un/acceptance
suburban strivings
I loudly renounced
to re/create
myself

So on
your evening of tribute
I bare witness
to families born/chosen connecting
cross borders once heavily/guarded
Over demarcations of personal/political
private life/public work
I hold breath
as disparate pieces fall
into place & see
that territories
are not separate
these lines were
artificially imposed

In mirrors
the faces of mother
brother/father stare back
When laughing
mummy's sarcastic cackle
resounds in my throat
I realize much of the me I/we have created
comes from them/comes in spite of them
comes/apart from them

T h r e e

The world
is full of believers
seeking media/messiahs/martyrs
to live life on a ledge/a public precipice
with communities below/entreating a
      jump
Invoking the names/Malcolm/
      Martin/Marcus

their Leader's
attributes/mythical
increase exponentially
with the number of years/after death
or fall out of fashion
like yesterday's dashiki

Fail
to recognize
leaders among/within/us
who aren't heterosexual/male
individualistic/self-aggrandizing
patriarchal/professional
captives of Robert's rules

Leaders
teach/nurture
collective skills/talents
consciousness/for change
and know when
to stop

We learn our politics
through the process of osmosis
Finding ourselves nodding heads
moaning deep in unison
as our words echo/in our ears
our verbal fingerprints
turns of phrase/issue forth
in a higher pitch/lower
from a brother/sister
with whom we share
ourselves

Wearing pants/you once owned
I watch you admire your old shoes/
    re-shod
on an ever-styling sistah's long brown feet
& note that this moment is/a metaphor

F o u r

We inherit
a complex language
of silence(s)
Tongues which effortlessly
navigate a terrain of:
teeth/cocks/nipples/pussy
anger/hypocrisy/lies
are still learning
primary syllables
of tenderness/& intimacy

Sometimes affirmations
are telegraphed/subliminally
in the spaces left between
words & gestures
We struggle to bring
emotion/experience to tongue
To name ourselves without
       apology/shame
To carry our business out
over steaming bowls of red-pea soup
without self-consciousness
For in the life
our language is truth
our truth is resistance

I remember
that you talk & listen

We plot private revolutions
in the blue light of late night talk
and info-mercials
Find sanity and sustenance
amid incoherent/streams of consciousness
We talk and listen

I trust
that even as our journeys diverge
time will be found to Imagine
more ways of realizing
the "possibilities of possibilities"
and of leaving behind more
than a pretty corpse
& a room full
of mourners

TERRITORIES

Territories/distinct/separate
Mapped out/in mines/minds
Coming together/deep
In the heart of the ghetto

They came in a van-load
via the valley/Don
This armada of dreadlocked sistas
(sisters spelt with an a/an a for African)
To the door of the man/the man with a Jag
who wanted no politics by poolside/
no talk of diseases/behind his portals/private
The dreadlocked sistas/like Columbus discovered what had existed
And let us commemorate 500 years of resistance/I digress
The dreadlocked sistas like Columbus discovered
what had existed in their absence/without their presence
The dreadlocked sistas discovered what had existed

Never seen so many men/Black
So many men/Black/in one space/at one time/in one groove
So many men/Black/In one space/basement/at one time/night/
In one groove/Queer/together dancing

Black men/basement men grinding
In the dark/against re-furbished suburban walls
Reverberating to the dance-hall din
Reggae fresh off the boat/booming in cushy Toronto suburbs
Shabba/Shabba/Shabba

Basement men/Black
Grind in suburban spaces/underground
In a dance-hall din/to reggae rhymes of eradication

Basement men/Black
grinding into each other/against suburban walls
Grind into desire/grind into need/grind into fear/
Oblivious to reggae rhymes of eradication
Holding each other/they merge
Stitches rubs Le Château/Drakkar Noir rubs Eternity for Men
Holding each other tight/they merge
Leaving no space for the holy ghost/or politics of inclusion

Basement men Black/grind with their eyes shut tight
Wishing away your presence at the top of the stairs sistas
Grind with eyes shut tight/oblivious to reggae rhymes of eradication
Bam/Bam
Wishing away your presence at the top of the stairs/mother/daughter/lover/sistas
Bam/bam
leaving no room for the holy ghost/or politics of inclusion
Bam/bam
Wishing away eyes bearing witness/tongues that might testify/of this silent fraternity
Bam/bam
Wishing away your presence at the top of the stairs sistas/your faces of community/cultural
Bam/bam
Wishing away your presence at the top of the stairs sistas/ your mouths naming
identities/shared
Bam/bam
Wishing away your presence at the top of the stairs sistas/your fingers pointing to
power/unequal
Bam/bam
Wishing away your presence at the top of the stairs sistas/
Bam/bam
It's a dick thang
(thing spelt with an a/an a for African)
Bam/bam
you wouldn't understand.

EARLY CONFESSION

I am/six/seven/years old
J.R./Uncle Magnus' first son
My eldest cousin from Spanish Town
came to Morant Bay/to spend the weekends
with his family in the country
Us

Saturday/barber day
Perched high on a board/hard
across the arms of the red vinyl chair
straight razor/sharp/drawn quick
against long black strap
swoops/swoops/swoops
heads shaved/shine/clean/peeled
a ritual ancient/frightening
My brother cried/
always

Saturday/market day
cacophonous crowds/
Gossip
'bout Miss Gwennie pickni/
or MassaSam who just come/from foreign
Higglers hawk goods
brought distances/far
on high head bundles/overburdened country buses
smell thyme bunches/nutmeg piled/bay leaf garlands/allspice
mingles with over-ripe fruit/rotting
in the sun

Sunday we are ironed/crisp
for Sunday school at the Anglican church
across from the local prison
Where inmates could be heard/
screaming obscenities/
even on Sunday

All things bright and beautiful
all creatures great and small
all things wise and wonderful
The Lord God made them all

Sunday/supper
Screeching fowl caught/beneath a wash-pan
Head/neck/pulled under the rim
and chopped off by my uncle's hand
lengthened by a sharp machete
Holding down the pan/
as the fowl danced/for life
severed head spewing blood
Sounds contained/muffled flappings silenced
it expired/ready
to be plucked/clean/
served with rice and gungo peas/
beetroot juice/sweetened with nutmeg
and condensed milk

Weekends/meant J.R.
We would find ourselves alone
in my great aunt's old wooden house
Aunt A. died years earlier
Her house stood/as it once did
furnished as she had left it
but emptied of her belongings/personal
her presence

J.R. and I
in the closed space of Aunt A's vacant home
behind doors/latched/under iron bed
spread with pale yellow chenille
Junior and I play sex/
as yet unnamed
Rubbing buddies/erect
maga bodies/hold each other
mimick movements/imagined
little penises/between underdeveloped thighs
motions rough/tender
Dusty chimmy bears witness
to pleasures/childish
Floorboards creak/as we roll
knock heads/exchange anxious/excited beads of sweat
Smelling of soap and powder/me
gamey pre-adolescence/him
we explored feelings/as yet unnamed
or completely understood
and kept silent
by instinct

GILL'S PARADISE

Crown Heights
Paradise found/Brooklyn block/crumbles
Through gypsy cab/Classon and Pacific streets
a hell/to eyes not seein' home/
On this neglect paved/urban artery
apathy's pothole/open hydrant/piss stained wall
street corners/"the Dream"

Burned-out shell/stands/three-stories
three sets of eyes/concrete sealed
willful/blind/remembers better days
Next door Gill's Paradise/is overpainted 'ho
gaudy yellow facade/single palm/Rastaman
and lion of Judah/testify to longings/distant/unfilled
romance defiant/in decay
Gill's beckons

Behind bars and heavy plastic/wicket woman's
painted fingers/grab green/currency
Thick man at door cops quick feel/searches
weapons/concealed
Pleasure's pre-payments made
upon entrance

First floor/
hot "house"
tropical speakers/steam beats
Black/orchids/bloom in a space safe/
climate uncontrolled/
We be styling/in shades/numerous:
bald-headed bangee boys/Kangol capped yardees/
dreadlocked racemen in kultural cloth/bodysuited activists/
closet buppies slummin'/denim and leathered downtown fags

foreign queers fleeing/boredom/each other
"The Man"/four hundred miles
from Colbys

We be
bubblin'/salty water beads
ricochet/across cast iron pan
sizzles/from closeness to desire/shared
We speak in motions primal/
other land language
grind/wine/batty-ride/tough/rhythms
forced so tight/up is the only direction
to dance
We be/secret tribe/nomads nocturnal
migrate from private space/to private space/
where blacked-out windows
extend nights into pelvic thrusts/
threaten to merge/two into one/
Man/hood from duplicitous shackles released
we flutter hands/finger pose/
like catwalk queens *"work it girl"*
fly furious/cross floors hard
with silence/in/visibility
We be caged birds freed
through unfurledwings/muscled limbs
wet with weekday toxins
Spins/snaps/sustained by ecstasy/Guiness stout
high/on fear of daylight's encroach
practicing the safest sex/fully clothed
dancin' on the edge

Outside bathed in neon/urban torches/we glow
Hangin' out in sonic booms/of auto discos
A soca flood/from dueling wombs
parked on opposite sides
engulfs
We be warm
Backed up against cars

and stiff-dicked buddies
in open air lounge
Spectate/on strutting parade
Pecks/pea-cocks/good 'ol Yankee ass
held high and proud/like Massi warriors
Gangsta gold glints/from open mouths/African mines/deep
spill protestations of love/scandalous jewels
in island twangs/unaffected
by estrangement/enforced
Major mandramas/happening
curbside

Glimpse/
a face/familiar
moonwalks/to Michael Jackson/re-mixed
lipsynchs lyrics/only he can hear
cross that line/fine
'tween survival/insanity
He's skinning teeth/blissful and mad
but "In the life"
still

Atmosphere/iced
Sober winds/blow
thoughts of lovers/who
have yet to be touched
We go hungry
surrounded by this ocular feast/of plenty
ground provisions for our/cultural consciousness/
Politically correct/libidos
awakened by purple lips/full
promisin' transitory passion/
whispering faint/tales of violence:
drive-by lovers/firing cusses/cold
"40-head" rudeboys/weaned on dance-hall anthems by Buju
flinging metal/rockstones
And bodies/left prone/
fucking asphalt

We pre/tend natives
depart this space
for territories un/familiar
Swagger like straight men
fists pocketed against the chill/
Three/alley boys/shooting up some shit/
doing a deal
whistle hollow as we pass/
three whistles/carry no tune
of longing/lust familiar
Pursed lips/expel air/damp
with con/fron/tation
We be stiff backed/steppin' short
for the underground "A"/uptown
Propelled/forward
As if chased by specters/shape shifters
bashing at our brazenness
Backs stiffen/steps short/fall/fast
in anticipation/of slur-tipped/phobic knives
jutting from the small of our backs/
In anticipation of feathered arrows/
from archers/looking like ourselves
bearing messages/un/gentle minders
that (we)
brother loving brothers
stepping out of shadowy/spaces/secret
threats to the status quo
Dance on the edge
of extinction

ON VIEWING MASALA

A chicken/eggplant/potato roti
came through my pores Tuesday morning
Through armpit's wetness
the stink of day old curry
fried in ghee/wrapped in flour
shared my bed and brought me back
to Ontario Housing
Lawrence Avenue's fourth floor corridors
thick walls/thin doors
Babies bawl/sirens
Spouses in combat/common-law
Canned laughter from the 26" Zenith
blares Starsky and Hutch/gunshots
Dirty carpets/seep/cooking odours
of foreign climes/Paki smells
they say

I remember
the building's backside
where "Fucking Nigger"
dropped to the pavement like gob
from a 12th floor balcony/dewdrops
out of unwashed/white mouths
twisted by minority status/newfound
Taunt lands near metal bins/cold/blue
full of refuse/immigrant dreams
in brown paper bags/denied/deferred

Brought me back
to the crowded Spadina bus/on a wet day
where passengers are close
smelling of raw fish/black beans/aggression
Chini smells
they say

And I remember you
Third storey walkup/Ossington/Bloor
above a donut/variety store
2am Saturday night/Sunday morning
on the street/The Somalian club disgorges
it's patrons/drunk and drawn
to our music/blaring out of open windows
Drunk and drawn to our faces
peering out for air and excitement
They/the new Black people
with motherland shapes/different hair
asserting attitude/speaking in tongues
To us old wave West Indians
Second generation Canadians
Children of the diaspora
connected to the continent only
by the medallions around our necks
the dash of Kente on our clothing
the mud cloth draped on our furnishings
They are drunk and drawn to our music
But Bob Marley is ours
Sorry, private party closed
cross culturally

Bored
we play truth or dare
with visions of Madonna and
that bottle of water
God! don't ask me anything
Don't ask me as you did Tom
how many lovers he has had
less than 100?/more than 50?
I can't imagine the faces/can he remember
the names/all those names
I remember our earlier game: "I'm so deprived ..."
and feel just that
Oh don't ask me truth
Truth frightens/reveals me
I can't lie well

Dare
Dare me to do a striptease/in the middle of the room
to Oleta Adams' Rhythm of Life
Dawmp/Dawmp/Dawmp/(to the tune of the song)
and I oblige/flashing chest hairs
bony shoulders/the band of my briefs
Calvin Klein/Calvin Klein/Calvin Klein
Dare
Dare you to kiss me
and you jump into my mouth
knock my teeth/slip in your tongue
when my eyes were closed
and thoughts hadn't time to form
Your mouth envelopes/like city heat
hot/damp/un-air conditioned
tasting not unpleasantly of dal
basmati rice/nicotine
or do I imagine this
But the last kiss
the last kiss
was real

All the same
4:45 Sunday morning
I hork/a horrible/real word
I hork at the side of the road
and expel your saliva/foreign
from my mouth

My friend a dreadlocked Dolly Levi
will not let me forget

"what a cute couple we make"
"Go ahead try a ting/try a ting"

On viewing Masala

TO BE/TO BE/AFRO-SAXON

To be/to be/Afro-Saxon
And shield myself beneath layers of tweed/myself
Paisley silk/slip knotted at my neck
Orphan child/of a movement
that gave access to a culture/seductive
A history of conquerors
helped me slip easily/out of my skin
My skin/lubricated by exclusion
I slip out of skin/enter bar
begin search for a man/The man
To make me forget
the nature of my pain/the depth of my loss/my need

I nurse a beer/sip/swallow
Rejection/bitter/yet warm
Walk the floor pressed onward by sounds/primal
Groped by crowds/in heat/ bodies/entangled in smoke
Avoid eyes dark/shining in corners
dimly illuminating angry inner fires
of educated erasure/and distancing fantasies/of Other
Avoid dark eyes/that never meet yours
Disconnected from faces
Bodily beacons of loneliness/loathing/loss

I turn away
And walk the circle/in circles/towards the light
And find myself wanted/not for the content of my character
"The man"/does not see/the me I have invented/from pieces scattered/broken
The me I have imagined/from fragments yet to be excavated
"The man's" eyes calibrate
the length of my dick
muses aloud about
the luster of my skin
and traces with his finger/my lips
He's seeking pleasure/collecting heads
looking for ass/to colonize

But his eyes are not dark/and do not reflect
the depth of my loss/the nature of my need
And he will help me forget/as we fuck
Amidst chintz/and fine literature
The depth of my loss/the nature of my need
And I will not remember until I am left alone/in daylight
The spaces that his cock/could not fill
And those dark eyes of memory.

CRAIG

was jumping/in Tracks/
capital T/D/C/Washington
carryin' on/makin' noise/being loud
in black and white/polka dotted pantihose
tight white tank top/matching canvas Keds/the slip on kind
dancin'/and cruising/in disco drag

He was/is drag/fierce drag
not just disco drag/but drag queen drag/suburban b-boy drag
radical drag/afrocentric drag/Lola Falana at Caesar's Palace drag
Angela Davis in the Panthers drag/even upwardly mobile/credit to his race/
Black business man drag of
Wall Street blue/pinstriped suits/
pale coloured shirts/rep-striped ties
Any costume/clothing
was drag

On his slight/brown frame/
Craig strutted/worked his drag/
not a camouflage/
but for visibility/high
Wore his id/intellect/identity
like he wore two-piece suits/
silk chiffon scarves/
and boyfriends
A sign/A shield
that protected/yet distanced
him from brothers who couldn't deal with out/outrageousness
'Cause it wasn't enough to be Black and Gay
Black and Gay/and fierce/you had to have politics
politics/and a high vq/visibility quotient

Fierce BGM with high v.q.
was seeking same/seeking same
Craig knew power
was in voice/
visibility
drag
Craig

CATHARSIS

Remember
Remember my name
David/Dwayne/Craig/Rory
David/Dwayne/Craig/Rory
At rest/at peace/gone home/pass away/steal away
Into the arms of the lord
Abide with me lord
Died

Where is
Where is the love?

The count begins
1/2/3/4
David/Dwayne/Craig/Rory
Man was not meant to lie with man
It is an abomination unto the lord

Where is
Where is the resting place/final
for the unrepentant faggot
who believed in the realness
of Diana Ross' hair
The saintly rasp of Lady Day
caught between heartache/and heroin
in the vinyl grooves/scratched and caught
God/God/Bless the child
We/I believed
And got on my knees/to thank the lord
for a body warm/with which to pass the terrors
of the night
Got on my knees to suck redemption
from a thickly veined shaft/of possibilities/endless

JEFFERY CONWAY

TO AN ANGEL

The first time we meet
in New York City
it will be snowing.
No one will stop
to take a picture
of us as we stand
inches apart and shake
hands on a busy street
corner. Taxicabs
will continue to pass,
splattering dirty slush
onto our wool coats.
We will walk
in silence to a café
where we'll sit
for hours sipping
espresso, fingering sugar
packets. The smoke
from your cigarette
will rise and hover
around your head
like mist in a grave-
yard covering
a tombstone at dawn,
the epitaph barely readable.
Just after midnight
you will lean forward,
your face—pale
and thin—emerging
from the haze, eyes
dark as skulls',
and slowly, unnoticed,
we will kiss.

TOMBSTONES

The snow glows outside
as white as hotel sheets in this dark
February. His bare back blocks the cold
air coming from the cracked window
like a warm stone. I'm thinking
about that bright day last August
when I followed him on my bike.
We rode past the Cape End Retirement Home
to the P-town cemetery. He parked
his blue Schwinn and I leaned
my borrowed brown Raleigh against it.
"This is a good place for wild flowers," he said,
rushing down a narrow path into the brush.
The wind came up, clouds moved across the sky.
I looked around: cheap vases, wilting
red carnations and ratty silk roses
adorned the graves. I followed and found him
standing in a clearing with a handful
of blossoming weeds. He smiled, held them out,
then pulled them close to his chest,
"You might be allergic."
I couldn't resist and grabbed his wrist:
our lips pressed for a moment.

Further down the trail we came across a mound
of discarded tombstones piled up like bones
behind an old shed. I watched as he pointed out
the treasures: this slab a great coffee table,
that one a good shelf, this broken piece a perfect trivet.
We rode our bikes to Herring Cove and walked
through clumps of beach roses to the sand.
We stripped down to our trunks and I led him by the hand
into the clear water. Or did he lead me?
Shall I wake him and ask? I can hear his breathing.
He's not absentminded, always attentive
to what he's doing. Yet, he resists remembering

dreams with the strength of an ox.
I'm not so strong. Yesterday, before
he got out of bed to put on a pot
of coffee, I rolled over and told him
I was on a stage in a fancy
hotel ballroom, a spotlight on my face.
Six old ladies in their eighties each
with a Bible in her lap sat at a round
satin-clothed table and stared as I read
a poem about how I trace the velvet vein
of his cock with my tongue, how I suck
his thick dick until it goes limp and hangs
like the pink roses on that P-town beach,
drooping, drunk from the afternoon glow.
The old women made crosses with their index
fingers and cut the spot. My father stood up
in the back of the room and shook his head,
"You said this was a poetry reading," and stormed
out the double doors marked EXIT. One old bag
threw her leatherette Bible and a hex:
"Turn or burn for having sinful sex!"
I stood alone on the stage and laughed,
"Turn or burn? I am a dragon—born in 64,"
and with that I opened my mouth and fire
poured out. I walked through the burning ballroom
like Carrie the night of her prom. I woke
myself up and my tongue hurt.
I recounted the dream to him with ease.

But tonight, as the wind blows ice and snow like sand
against the window, and as this lovely man falls deep
into sleep much like a statue might,
it seems risky to write in burgundy ink
about that day we stood and kissed
near a heap of tombstones at the tip of the Cape.

WEIGHT BELT

For Russell Falcon
b. Nov. 1955 d. May 1987

What I know of you I take
from three old photos buried in a leather box
in a corner of my lover's living room.
What I know of you I take
from stories, stories I receive
like communion, in silence with awe:
the first time he ever laid eyes on you
in a crowded room in New York City,
he stopped dead and couldn't move,
had to be pulled away by the shirt collar;
the time you cut his hair
at his apartment, slowly your hands
made their way from his scalp
down his nose to his lips,
the scissors fell to the floor
and you began to kiss, even though
it was forbidden—you'd been seeing his best friend.

In one photo you are achingly sexy—
you stand on a beach in a tight swimsuit,
head cocked to one side, thick build, black
hair, mustache. In another you are partner
to the one I love, sitting a step higher than him
on the porch of a P-town house.
The third I think of most often: you are emaciated
in the stark white tub
in the apartment on Sixteenth Street,
your face drained, beaded with sweat,
your dark eyes glassy marbles.

It is June and I've fled New York,
but still you find me here on the Cape.
You come to mind by design, the way
birds would appear along the path
in front of Jackie O. as she strolled
the grounds of her private retreat—
the papers said her gardener secretly walked
ahead, tossing seed on the trail.

Today I crossed the breakwater
to deserted Long Point Beach, spread my towel
and drifted asleep. I woke feeling something—
a caterpillar—crawling on my thigh.
I scooped it up with the toy shovel
I'd found earlier, carried it to the dune,
and set it free on a stalk of beach grass.
I returned to my towel and watched as the black
fuzz zigzagged back towards me,
scrunching itself up and out.
I picked it up once more,
tossed it into the dune. Again it inched
towards me. And right then
my thoughts turned to you. I shoveled
that caterpillar up, hurling it as far as I could,
then went for a swim in the icy water.

On my way home across the rocks,
I ran into a friend who stopped me
to say how lucky I am to have such a nice man.
He said, "I knew his ex, Russell.
He was the sweetest angel."
I mumbled goodbye and stormed off.

Later I biked to the gym
and put on your weight belt,
the one he gave me months ago, saying
someone should make use of it.
I slipped the silver tongue
into the hole I carve for myself each day—
a notch tighter than the one worn in by you.
I stared at my body
in the glitzy mirrors; too thin, I thought,
and pushed the dumbbells into the air.
I felt the pressure of black leather
on my sides and lower back. It held me
like a pair of strong hands, the way
your hand, veiny and soft, clutched a pen—
the day I took the belt he told me
that you began to write a lot toward the end.

SISTER

What else do you do in the afternoons, Cindy,
besides lying on the shredded sofa, hung over,
too tired to reach for another novel
settling, instead, for a reread
of the one in front of you, too tired
to tend to your brain-damaged baby
in the next room who, I've been told,
has red hair, unlike the twins
who were supposed to be fair
after you told everyone, anyone
an Irish man was the father
everything wrecked when they came out
quadroon, not at all like him or you, really
and what do you do when no one will have you
are you pregnant again or have the abortions
made it impossible, beyond repair
like the scare Mother gave you
holding up your dirtied underwear
in front of us all then cutting your hair
how come you didn't cry, how come
when I pick up the phone
and call you to ask I can't speak
I open my mouth and dead things fall out

SESTINA TO A TATTOOED BOY

We were talking. He said, "Excuse me," and asked the bartender for a glass
of red wine. This seemed strange for a boy
like him: ripped jeans, shaved head, and a tattoo of an angel on his perfect ass—
something I discovered later, after I'd lit three candles in my dark
bedroom. He stripped by flickering light and removed the safety-
pin from his right ear; his skin glowed like milk.

I offered him a drink. He whispered, "I'm dying for some milk."
I was drunk; my liver ached. In the kitchen I poured myself a glass
of aloe vera juice—it helped the pain inside. To be safe,
I drank two that night, hoping I wouldn't vomit booze all over the boy
in my bed. Shaking, I carried the quart of milk down the dark
hallway, opened the door to my room, and sat my ass

down on the futon. He rolled over and we kissed. There was a loud crash: "You ass-
hole!" My roommate, Michael, was screaming. I jumped, knocking the milk
carton to the floor, then fumbled my way through the dark
apartment and pushed open his door. *Heart of Glass*—
a warped tape—was playing. William, Michael's ex-boy-
friend, had picked the front door lock like a thief cracking a safe.

He'd taken his clothes off outside. "Let's fuck," he screamed, "unsafe
sex only, baby—no rubbers, let's get some ass—
everyone gets a piece—I can smell my boy's
ass anywhere!" I punched him in the nose, blood spattered like the milk
on my bedroom floor. Michael yelled, "Get out!" and threw a glass
vase containing a dead, dark

red rose. Someone was hiding in the dark
under the covers in bed. Michael ordered, "Stay there till it's safe."
I shoved William towards the door. He cut his foot on broken glass,
turned on me screaming, "Come on, I'll kick your ass!"
His blood on my hand felt like warm milk.
He took a step. "Hey Michael," he hissed, "does that boy

in bed with you know you've got AIDS?" The boy
beneath the blanket didn't move. Everyone was silent in the dark
bedroom. I threw William into the street. Rain poured like milk
from the drain pipe, drenching his pile of clothes. I slammed the door. Safe
inside my bedroom, I found the boy with the tattooed ass
up and dressed. "Don't go," I begged. "The milk—let me pour you a glass."

I ran to the kitchen, rinsed the aloe vera from my glass. When I returned, the boy
was gone. Still drunk on my ass, I fell to the bed and passed out in the dark.
The next morning I found the boy's safety-pin on the floor, in a pool of spilled milk.

HANGOVER

In a dark bar corner we talk for about an hour.
I drink Budweiser, he's sipping Miller Lites.
He leans over, kisses me—dark eyes, the most
handsome man I've seen—and invites me to his apartment.

In the cab he says my hands are rough, like a laborer's.
I say his are smooth, the hands of a statue.
"That's funny," he says, "I'm a sculptor."

We undress to the B side of The The's *Mind Bomb*.
I lie nude on top of him in bed. I'm drunk—slobbering as I kiss.
He says he'll get a rubber. I tell him no, I don't fuck.
He says we'll be really safe. I say no, I don't do that.
His cat jumps onto the bed, purrs. We pet her for awhile
then start to kiss again. We cum at the same time,
he pulls my body next to his without washing off.

At noon, after a few hours sleep, he brings me tea
and oat bran cereal, banana sliced over top.
My head is pounding and I have a dry mouth.
I set the tray on the floor, kiss him again.
We cum a second time. The tea is cold when I reach for it
and the cat has licked the milk from my bowl.
Next to the tray on the floor I see a card
from the Spike, where we met. I turn it over—"Phil"
and a phone number, 201 area code. New Jersey?

At the door, "Thank you for having me over."
He takes an orange from the off-white fruit bowl in the kitchen,
kisses it, puts it to my lips, then slides it into my hand,
telling me to take it for the subway ride.

On the street, cold air—my eyes water.
The skin on my face is burned, his morning stubble.
I go down into the subway station at Houston and 2nd to wait for the F.
A Puerto Rican boy with dark eyes walks up, says he'll give me
$20 for the leather jacket I'm wearing. I say I bought it
in Tijuana, that I'm attached to it. He hands me a brown bag.
Inside there's a bottle of medicine for stomach ache and nausea.
He asks if I think it'll work, that he feels like barfing.
"It's worth a try," I say. He says he'll buy the orange
off me for a quarter, he's hungry. As the train pulls up
I say, "You can have the orange." I step in and watch him
devour the fruit as the doors close.
The train begins to rumble into a dark tunnel.

TUESDAY NIGHT

I'm having sex with a man I've never
met before in a room with two single
beds when Elizabeth Taylor stumbles in
drunk. The man tells me to hide under
one of the beds, so I do. Liz plops
down on the mattress I'm under and it sags,
pressing against my back. She giggles
then passes out. The man and I go
outside and get into an elevator
at the base of a tree house. As we ride
up, the man tells me I'm handsome, says
he'd really like to give it to me safe
in an armpit. I don't say anything,
but the idea of him giving it to me
in an armpit repulses me. We get off
on the 66th floor and I unlock
double doors with a key that's in my pocket.
The doors look just like the ones
to Uncle Bill's glamorous apartment
on *Family Affair*. Sure enough,
turns out this penthouse apartment is mine.
The man is real excited by the view
of the city and the nuclear power plants
spewing orange smoke in the distance.
He adores the lavish furnishings: plush
throw-rugs, glass tables, large white couches.

I'm not so excited, though. I'm wondering why
I decided to move into such an expensive place,
a place I don't seem to even like much; the ceilings
aren't high enough, there are too many walls
and the windows have aluminum frames.
The man starts to kiss my neck passionately,
traces my sketchy veins with his tongue.
"No! No!" I yell, pushing him away.
"This is all wrong, this just isn't me."
He grabs my hand, tells me to relax
and whispers in my left ear (the pierced one):
"'Come back often, take hold of me in the night,
when lips and skin remember ...'" I feel faint;
how does this man dressed in a suit and tie
know my favorite Cavafy line?
I sit in an overstuffed turquoise armchair.
He offers me a drink. "Seltzer," I say,
"with a twist." He hands me a 5th century
Grecian urn. I feel guilty about drinking
from something so valuable.
The man tells me not to worry, I can
afford it. I finish my drink and tell him
I'm leaving, I must check on Liz—
she might be sick. He says I'm just like all
the rest and to go ahead, walk out. So I do.

WHERE THE MOOD STRUCK ME

Front seat of my '67 Mustang at 55 MPH on the northbound 405 Freeway in the
   San Fernando Valley
My Northridge apartment in 106 degree heat
A lifeguard stand on Venice Beach at 3:00 AM
A 4th floor Venice Beach apartment overlooking the boardwalk
On Mr. Toad's Wild Ride at Disneyland
My '67 Mustang parked on a side street near the Odyssey night club in West Hollywood
Will Roger's State Beach at midnight
A tree house in the backyard of an old Hollywood estate
A guest house in Hollywood just off Sunset Blvd.
My apartment on Sunset Blvd.
Back end of my brother's truck parked on a dead-end street in North Hollywood
My dorm room the first year of college
An apartment with a view of the capitol in Sacramento, California
The apartment I shared with James for years just off Melrose Ave.
The house I shared with James for many months in the Hollywood Hills
The jacuzzi of that house
A Redondo Beach apartment near the ocean
A West Hollywood apartment just off Santa Monica Blvd.
A Hollywood apartment that overlooked the Hollywood Freeway
A cabin in Big Sur
A hotel room in San Francisco
A Manhattan apartment on the 45th floor
A "glory hole" room at The Cock Ring bar in Amsterdam
A hotel room in Amsterdam

Another hotel room in Amsterdam

Another hotel room in Amsterdam

A moving sidewalk in the Paris Metro in the middle of the night

An apartment in Paris

Another apartment in Paris

The bunker where Hitler committed suicide in Berlin

A dark room at bar "Crisco" in Florence

A Manhattan apartment on the Upper East Side

My apartment in Chelsea

Another apartment in Chelsea on the same street

A SoHo apartment

A dark room at the Rapp Arts Center in the East Village on Halloween

A portable john in the parking lot of a Catholic high school in the East Village on New Year's Eve

An East Village apartment

My East Village apartment

A hotel room on the island of Maui every day for a week

A hotel room in San Luis Obispo

A hotel room in Carmel

A hotel room in Palm Springs three nights in row

Another hotel room at the same hotel in Palm Springs three more nights in a row

A condo in Ventura, California

A parking lot near a porno bookstore in Santa Barbara

A hotel room at the Ritz Carlton in Laguna Beach

Will Roger's State Park on a Sunday afternoon near a creek

A bathtub at Nancy's house in Brentwood

A jacuzzi next to the tennis court in the backyard of a Beverly Hills mansion

A house in Laurel Canyon

A Porsche parked on a side street near The Probe bar in Hollywood at 6:00 AM

My apartment on Dunsmuir Ave. in Los Angeles

In the dunes at Jones Beach just before a rain storm

A restroom in a DC-10 32,000 feet above the Grand Canyon

A railroad flat in the East Village

A house next to a bird sanctuary on Nantucket Island

The back porch of that house

Top of a rock at The Garden of the Gods in Colorado Springs

Room 8 at the White Horse Inn in Provincetown, Massachusetts

Back seat of a taxi headed down Houston St. in a snow storm

On the hull of a shipwrecked boat along the shore of Cape Cod

The "honeymoon suite" of a gay inn in a "gay" town in Maine

The second floor of a nineteenth century farm house in Kerhonkson, NY

In the bathroom on the first floor of that house

Ron's cottage on Cottage St.

Errol Flynn's deserted estate in the Hollywood Hills on a Friday night

A cemetery in Hollywood at dawn

FALL IN TOMPKINS SQUARE PARK

The homeless man slouched on a bench a few feet away screams
"She's thunder and I'm lightning, yes yes yes, thank you folks ..."
He's drinking T-Bird from the green bottle. I'm sitting with Ed.
We talk some, but mostly stare off into the trees (the leaves
are yellow and gold). "This is amazing!" I say. "We don't get this in L.A."
"Get what?" "The colored leaves." Ed is eating sunflower seeds.
"Well, I'm from New York," he says—spit—"and it's still fuckin' amazing."
A boy, 5 or 6, rides up in his red battery-operated car and parks
in front of us. He stares. Ed grumbles, "Hasn't he seen fags before?"
I'm thankful I won't have any kids—I couldn't stand so many questions,
they're always asking questions. At least I did: "Christ—are you writing
a book?" my mother would say with a cigarette stuck in her mouth,
her lips thin and red—no, orange—one of her favorite
lipstick colors, especially this time of year, *her* autumn in California:
Santa Anna winds, lounging by the pool, Tree-Top apple juice with vodka,
and the brown Oldsmobile wagon with fake wood-grain siding that she'd
drive at night, windows down, eyes bulging out, listening to AM radio.

BLOOD

Handel's *Messiah*
playing loud
on the stereo,
a pot of herb tea
cooling on the night-
stand, winter
sunlight illuminating
our eyes—blue, hazel;
we were kissing,
I hadn't shaved
in four days—
he had the morning
before and cut
his upper lip.
I guess my stubble
opened the wound
but we didn't notice
until he spotted drops
of blood on my cheek
and T-shirt. "I'm bleeding
on you!" he said,
jumping up, darting
into the bathroom.
He returned with a bottle
of hydrogen peroxide.
"Wash your mouth
out with this, quickly."
I swished the solution
around in my mouth
my gums burned
and bubbled.
He sat at the end
of the bed, rubbed
the nape of his neck.
"I haven't been tested—
you never know ..."
I walked to the bathroom
and spit into the sink.

FIRE ISLAND: July 3, 1990

The most handsome are blooming with strange diseases.
—Jean Genet

The boat sputters into the harbor at noon,
right on time. My friend Jerry waits for me on the dock, his right hand
waves in the air. I carry the purple
flower I bought in Manhattan—a perfect iris—
a duffel bag, copy of Sexton's *Live or Die*, and my old "Save the Whales"
sweatshirt. My first visit: the island is covered by clouds.

Jerry and I walk the small wooden boardwalk to his house—the humidity
is unbearable. He says, "Throw your stuff in the bedroom, we'll eat later tonight
by the pool, it'll be cooler then." I'm sweating like a pig—
hair sopping, jeans stuck to my thighs.
I change into cutoffs, dying to hit the beach. A lily
in the vase on the kitchen table smells incredible: I stop to sniff—it's pure white.

On the dirt path to the water I trip and cut my ankle on a grey
stone, complain to Jerry about the wilderness. It starts to rain.
Jerry tells me the cute little plant with the three shiny leaflets I fell into is poison ivy.
As we walk a couple miles along the shore the storm moves on; the afternoon
sky clears. I'm thankful there's no sign of a rash on my legs.
We reach Cherry Grove and turn back toward The Pines. We come across a beautiful deer

on the trail. As we move closer we see that it's gangling, covered with spots. "Ticks,"
Jerry says, "have given the island deer Lyme disease." The animal's black
eyes are glossy like marbles. Men are cruising nearby in the bushes. I stick my hand
out, but the deer runs, its ratted fur illuminated by shards of sunlight
filtering through the pine trees. I look at my watch, soon it'll be dusk.
I want to reach the house before dark—this trail is eerie, bordered by drooping daisies.

Jerry stops along the way, motions me over. We peer through a fence; a large bougainvillaea
is in full bloom—deep burgundy—inside the backyard. A toy poodle
yaps on the other side. A Latin guy in a black Speedo lounges by the pool, evening
shadows darken his face. The sliding glass door opens and a blond emerges from the blue
house; he kneels down and kisses the Latin boy. A cool breeze
makes the blond shiver; he dives into the clear water—we see that his back and neck

are covered with brown lesions. "K.S.," Jerry says. "It spread to my ex-lover's lungs
and killed him." The blond stands in the shallow end; his head dangles like a top-heavy rose
on a stem that bends. I tell Jerry I want to walk near the waves.
We turn away from the fence and follow the seagulls
to the sand. All the way back to the house my feet slosh through brown
sea foam. At home we eat pasta and bread, I do the dishes. Jerry's tired, says, "Good night."

The bars in town must be pumping, but I go for a midnight swim. My body
glows white in the pool as I walk down the smooth steps, arms out-stretched like vines,
palms up, legs itching—I'm thankful no jellyfish can attack. The sky is completely cloudless.

HIV

On Saint Mark's Place
Michael tells me
about the apartment
with high ceilings
and marble tub
he can't wait to get
in Paris someday
when he looks like
Liz Taylor, but older
and not as fat.
We laugh,
he grabs the Bud-
weiser out of my
hand and takes a
sip, keeping the can
away from his lips
because earlier he
complained about
bleeding gums—
the doctor said
he should be careful
about passing
it that way.

PHOTO

Walking east on East
4th Street I passed
an entrance to a grey
building and noticed
a photo of two nude men,
one on his knees sucking
the other's dick, torn
from a porno magazine
and pinned to the door.
A few more steps
and I turned around—
I wanted to have it.
But a girl walked up,
put a key into the lock
of the door, saw the photo,
ripped it down and threw
it on the sidewalk.
I passed her and glanced
at my watch, pretending
I was concerned about time.
A few feet away I stopped
and she disappeared
into the building. A hand-
some man in a suit bumped
me—my fault, "Excuse me."
I watched as he strolled
past and his eyes locked on
the photo lying there

on the ground. He
paused a moment, reached
down, picked it up
and carried it in his hand.
I followed him to the corner
and started to get hard
dreaming about his thoughts,
his hand, my heart
pounded faster as he'd glance
down at the photo, then up
at the flashing "DON'T
WALK," then back
down at the photo.
I waited.
He looked around and dropped
it into a metal trash can
on the curb, then crossed
the street against the light.
I walked over and picked
the photo out of the can,
and folded it into the right
rear pocket of my jeans.
The white "WALK" sign
appeared, so I walked.
My erection was gone
by the time I reached
the other side of the street.

FRIDAY NIGHT IN THE EAST VILLAGE

Alone in my apartment,
bored stiff. Change
the radio station
from Country to Rap,
Rap to Rock, turn
it off. Pull *The Face*
from bookshelf:
Morrissey; March, 1990.
Flip the pages.
Manchester's so hip;
I thought that
when I bought it,
but tonight it's a fright
(two years later
and I'm still
behind the times).
Look in the mirror:
I hate my hair.
Over to the window—
car alarm, siren, screams.
Plop down on the couch,
pick up the new *Interview*.
Marky Mark (I heart him)
on the cover, and a spread
on Brad Pitt!
He's going to Amsterdam
for a month:

"Yeah, I rented
this place on a canal.
One whole wall
is windows." *Please*.
Throw the rag
to the floor.
There's a new
fast-food chicken place
downstairs. Their
ventilation duct runs
up the back
of the building
to a huge fan
on the roof.
This is 5E,
the top floor—
the whole apartment
is humming.
I need to clean
the bathroom.
Exene is curled up
in a tight ball
at my side. God,
the radiator's hissing
up a storm.
The lights just flickered—
I'm in the dark.

R.M. VAUGHAN

CULTIVATING THORNLESS ROSES
OR, 5 CONVERSATIONS ABOUT ANAL SEX

preparing the soil

he said   have you been a good boy ? and I said is it Saturday night (no, it's not)
he said   have you been my best, best boy? and I said is my name Robert (sometimes)   he said
    with all the malice 2 years of community college acting class and one
    television commercial for the Beef Marketing Board gave him sense memory for
have you had it up the ass   lately   pal?   and I said why no not in ever so long (I promise
you)
so he asked   can you drive I'm drunk?   and I opened my eyes again and said no, actually, no
    (the truth,   and both of us amazed)   —   not bad for   a Tuesday, at not even 10:30, so close to
(his) home   roommates away—

    inside the darker muscle, the part you know is not red   but could be crimson
if exposed to light   so much heat   I read somewhere you can cook
an egg up your ass, it's the bile, the acid
        he will melt in there and the latex, a hated winter coat

choosing the right hybrid for your temperate zone

      please remember that hardwood floor is not eiderdown and cartilage is not muscle
forgive me if I feel less urgent on my knees than my natural submissiveness and half an hour ago
suggest
      maybe the combination of   Nivea cream, only it smells of mint and sulphur   plus
an angora cat named Tickles   plus your devotion to liberal causes
destroys my proposal that you are always on top and lift weights only to release stress and
have no hair care products except beer shampoo
   clean, I feel stupidly clean   in the dirtiest place on the body
   it must be the opening and stretching   the making room   some trick with oxygenation
bubbles in the blood

well after all danger of frost is passed

    no telling about cocks. Cocks do not correspond to body shapes   (big ass,
skinny dick—I've seen it once I've seen it   so many times)   they're covered for a reason
    no telling about cocks, cocks and posture   some of the most upright citizens I know
bent like coathangers, and the cleverest dicks—perfect fish gill ribbing, platform heads, fat
as a neck—still stumble out of zippers   so unpracticed

for instance your backbone, of North American grade   like Gary Cooper in The Fountainhead
surprising you can move at all (except forwards)   but, pants down, caught my thighs

    I could swear   double jointed
    in, in fast and low and fast and crooked   vertical—90 degrees to the last link
in my spine   an index finger making letter C, or a weed, stubborn between flatstones

pruning

remember it's rubber   cold and clean   slick as water, only harder and no
you can't be allergic: rubber is clean, it comes from trees, it's ecological
    now, unsnare your shoulders, lower the jaw   breathe from the stomach   1,2,1,2,1
2   the whole lower body comes unglued
    shhh   no,   only rubber—   OK the pink colour isn't natural who knows what colour rubber
is when it spills through the bark I wasn't there   it can't hurt you, rubber is a complex protein
is this a trust issue?

    —   2,1, 2, 1, 2   1   my lungs are not in my ass   this backwards LaMase technique
feels like drowning in dry air, my whole sex life flashing past me   ending with you
2, 1, 2,   1 of the quickest ways to make me tense is the word Relax   and tires are rubber
and tires can kill you tires can lift you off the street   make you   fly
into stop signs, arc over shop windows   crush small children when you land   run over your foot
tires can —

stop, see   it's in   see? touch down here, lower—round peg fits in almond (same circumference)
it's a science   it's breaking the rules   like rubber is a liquid and a solid all at once   like ice or
breath on car windows or anything you eat cold

    remember the old dentist's trick   ask a complex question, hit the nerve

American beauty rose

now for one of the few carnal pleasures in which freshness is not an issue

a careful shave with mirror on the toilet seat, razor head knocking backwards, slack, backwards
index and thumb tight, like pinching salt   only a little blood (such careful times)

later, together   will a warm, hairless rub   loosen tendons ? no   does the pink
(from lack of sun)   on blush   (razorfresh)   bring out the garnet centre? yes, a little

folded together a clutch of muscles shapes inconclusive smirks, the kind two or three knotted
petals make in half opened buds
        from so much compression   (of pigment, essential oil,
        the gummy undersides of leaves)   a red fist   hard,   for fighting

can a clean shave frame a violent act, the way I trust straight teeth, new shoes? or apologize
for an interruption   with childish murmurs, with innocence—I wasn't born with hair
down here—

a shaved asshole is a little lie

for the not few pleasures in which freshness is now an issue   we improvise

10 REASONS WHY I FALL IN LOVE WITH INACCESSIBLE STRAIGHT BOYS EVERY DAMN TIME

1. cause when he laughs at my jokes or tells me he likes my clothes it can't be anything but the truth and if you're a fag you know what I mean.

2. straight boys speak a foreign tongue I never learned—a semaphore of scruffy chin tugs, bearish shoulders, and dead dog easy posture. straight boys can spit, far, and seem to like urinals.

3. a straight boy will always hate opera and will never, ever play some god-awful Whitney Houston record before he feels you up on the couch—straight boys like guitars.

4. cause foreign films are for girls with glasses or nervous Anglican boys who went to private school—and Yes, Thank You, he does eat meat.

5. straight boys don't trust their fathers either.

6. a straight boy will wear a tight tee-shirt no matter how fat he is. I call this Innocence.

7. OK, yes, even if he does have three kids and two monthly car payments and at least one house he still has more money than most of the fags I know and Money = Relaxation.

8. cause once I went to the Y and I swear to God four straight boys massaged each other buck naked and talked about body fat ratios and not one got hard or even a little glassy-eyed and I knew, I knew I was on another planet and I have always wanted to see the stars up close.

9. straight boys remind me of children—big, hapless, grown up children with sex organs it would be right and legal and far more interesting to touch.

10. because women don't really trust them anyway so they'd be better off with me.

DOCTORS FAUSTUS

Drs. Faustus #1

underhand
     a calfskin case swings on the hook
          of his finger
black, hand-tooled
—a pendulum testing the pit
of my stomach—
it clicks clean   shut and open
     clean as tapshoes on pine   unresonant, predetermined

inside   (withheld) results match hopeful numbers
to manly romances   serials
     plotting want, quick fixes   lean denouements
     melodramas of plus or minus

all   but stripped
a coarse paper coverlet spread flat across the mantel
    of my lap
is only protocol
in an office as hot as summer tea
     —a gentleman's white glove, a sauna towel

it would be pointless to cry in here, throw water on the (hot) rocks
     exchange fluid to gas (get steamed)
make the room close
for everybody else

... downtown
     a hundred briefcases punch my thighs
     smelling fear.

Drs. Faustus #2

take the lead, bring it up   pull tight
        shut eyes open   now
put your finger on the knot
in my throat   and press
        me for an answer   (string me along)
while my arms are tied in a bow across my chest
    (cat's cradle)
        ... our push-me-pulley game of resistance and (long) waits

every day is Christmas for you
so much unwrapping
I can't see the floor   for paper

make the loop, bring the end through
                    it again   let's go   through
you I'm remembering what I'm here to lose
                a stitch in my belly, an unravelling
            spool never regains its composure
            never looks as whole
                    hour's gone by, here's a little something
to tie me over

Drs. Faustus #3

on the hard-earned desk stand three flat squares of dulled brass
      a son   a wife   a boat at sea
                                  (the *Laissez Fair*)
on the slink-backed pink chair   three feet from the hull
                                (spitting distance)
I'm telling your best doctor no face   I need
      two of the reds and one of the oranges   a day   please

      shift your weight, lean in to the lesson
          at your spread hands   today
        I'm everyone who needs   a talking to
      a son   a wife   a body
                    seized

legs uncrossed, your hand-pressed slacks   lint-pill   at the crotch
like cheap seat covers
      eyes down, lips smirked, I'll listen   now

      there's only chemistry   between us
      and power.

Drs. Faustus #4

"... now, I've been in this game a long time"

      a history of medicine is a history of poison
"and, between you and me, it's always a case"

      of trial and horror
      so much of it   merely a wringing of hands
          sheet changes   tendered mercies
      making me confrontable

"I've known you since you were so tall"

          I'm supposed to find comfort in that
      "I see this every day"
      (nod, suggest maybe it's nothing)
"In an ideal world we would cure ourselves"
               but I can't, so make it easy

"know our own bodies"
      but I don't, so do your job
            "make our own medicines"
      God   yes   eliminate the middle man
"exercise, eat right"
      shut up   shut up   shut up

"not take a pill for every little thing"
              I need is in that bottle   you bastard

"know that we're all important in our own"
            you're of no importance

"I don't like to do this, but I guess it's too late"

          once the bottle's opened

Drs. Faustus #5

I can start screaming   just you try me

—hollering, bellowing, caterwalling   madness
          not this stifled sob-catching bit o' blues   soft as candles
under hot lamps   but a hard, lacquer hard   carapace
     between me
and theory
I   and the interrogative
   sound   and inflection.

A THIN MAN

approaches me from a black-lit corner
smelling of dancefloor sweat, hips tick-tocking
against the air (as if it resisted)—in line and step
with the thud and swirl of this season's rage,
a mimic shadow tracing a dozen feisty trunks of boys half his age moving
twice as fast   (blocking my view)

he wants a match,
a stick of sulphur and pressed paper to carry
back into the purplish light that recognizes only florescence
and white
I overlook his magic lantern show of lummette before cigarette before face
        my eyes, trained to the floor, on the dance,
        knew that he had seen
        nothing more could come
        from me.

3 POEMS FOR PAUL BOWLES

1. paul and jane

... names from children's readers
       or English colouring books
work-a-day   saints' names   hung on the back end of hyphens
              like afterthoughts
names tired mothers give their fifth or seventh child

... all grown up and an ocean away, we nap   spines cool
       against whitewash and aqua tile   beds apart
    sexes (punch and judy)   dumbed by 2 pm heat
    we share (only) alike dreams
of Tangiers afternoons under lovers like ourselves (not the other)
of sweating pigments of brown and white and common red
of curing   two skins
       the colour of unleavened bread.

2. *dit moi, m' mohammed*

car   je vu une journée trop long   mais seulment
          un fragment d'un roman, mon roman   tous le même
dit moi
où est la table, la tasse, le kif, les pages?   tous les periodes, grains
inscriptions   pour mon histoire?
                 sûr ta peau ...

m' mohammed   tu as trois femmes et deux hommes
                 à le vers entre ton menton et ta aine
                 comme la Shiva, comme un ver
m'mohammed   tes levrès sur ma sexe, nôtre peau marron   par nature où
          par choix   dit moi   *je t'aime*   où
quelques chose.

3. the tired place

in the sun, how long I've walked   for stories, a bed
   ... but rest—it too shuns   still asks to see my papers, calls my hand

some men spit, look away   make noises in the souk
      a slow language
with tongue and water and billowed cheek   (semaphore)
      call me *reguiba blanc*
ask me home

          after mint tea, black cigarettes   always rough mouthing,
          slicked thighs, maybe fists

         ... everything gets written down, beds are rolled for travel
eyes shut   like it or not.

from SICKNESS LEXICON

1. refuse

The first bowl of blood arrived
unannounced, a toxic spill,
more orange than red;
slick, precipitous,
oil on brine—
a wash of lurid watercolour
marring the white gesso
of the toilet.
As if, by proxy, (but not behalf)
my body had voted
against me and my
continuation,
against
my term,
my office,
my presidency for life.

I read the quiet, brilliant curls
of iron, water,
and salt,
prophetically, like tea leaves:
the powdery tissue
my folded,
parchment square;
the simple exchange, from vessel
to vessel,
of excess,
my Lottery;
the flamenco smear
my black dot
        and I whispered,
"I'm made of stronger stuff than this

        somewhere."

4. actuality/virtuality

Quietly,
in a restaurant
of your choice
I sit
impaled on a polished fork spine,
my blood dressing the leafy
pine-green salad,
(a Camille, draped in Aunt Jemima linen)
and take your order:
tonight Monsieur will play
the beloved
and I his host
for the evening—

I expect to be tipped.

On your floor,
my eyes bulging
like harvest breasts,
I acquiesce:
beg forgiveness, beg
for more;
my simple lust always ready, like my ass,
to be victimized.
We fuck
like two accountants:
charge/countercharge, balance
and weight,
pencil and pen,
investment and residence:
gasping, I generously produce a down of sweat,
you position your
self
and again, we read from our scripts—
two neck's millstones
of education, necessity, and promise—
and play
father to daughter,
brother against brother,
Tortoise versus Hare.

7. all I want to say is

if you cannot cure me
shut up.
if you cannot ease my pain
just shut up.
if you are afraid of me
leave my house.
if you wanna fight
put   em   up,
cause   I've   got   nothing left
to lose.
if you are tired
of my complaining
stop tracing
my calls.
if you want to live to see
me and mine
planted, 6-deep
good as gone—
run
as fast as you can
before I choke your neck
with my barren
hands.

3 POSSIBLE TITLES FOR A POEM ABOUT ANIMALS OR WHY I DO NOT REGRET MY ACTIONS IN GRADE 11 BIOLOGY

1. The Crass Menagerie

in The Little Girl Who Lived Down The Lane   starring Jodie Foster and Martin
Sheen   Martin butts a smoke in Jodie's hamster's face and there's the most
pathetic tinned whoopy cushion scream and the hamster (or is it a gerbil?) hits
the coals   on the fireplace   a sound engineer taped the snap of frying bacon
for continuity

maybe because not even a pedophile cop too short for lead roles and bigger
budgets
could   toss a golden retriever   a tabby   a minor macaw
into Hell   just to find out if Jodie killed her father (he's buried downstairs)
what we have here is *cinema verité*

or

no, sir   I can't do
he's still   (OK she) moving
yes, actually, I want to be different than the rest of the boys (under my breath)
          forever

2. 101 Damnations

I'm sorry, I can't afford cruelty-free products.
I'm sorry, but, I simply cannot afford cruelty-free products.
I really am sorry I wish I could afford your fine selection of cruelty-free products.

(repeat 98 times)

        In 1976 I stayed for five days with my Aunt Ethel in Greenwich,
Connecticut and I believed from her back balcony you could see the Empire
State Building   it only took patience

I forgive Santerians for sacrificing live chickens and goats. It's part of their
culture.
I overlook Kosher slaughter practice (bleeding to death). It's part of Jewish
culture.
I respect the inherent rights of First Nations people to hunt at their leisure. It is an intrinsic
component of their culture.

(repeat 98 times, with variations)

        In late summer 1976 my Aunt Ethel told me in three short slaps of her voice   grown up
boys no longer sleep at night with their mothers
(grown up boys get the couch)
        spend good Canadian money on Fonzi stickers (they build models, which are educational)
        impersonate Grover or Ernie or The Wonder Twins (rots the mind)

and the Empire State Building hung just outside my range, it only took focus
squinting   the right winds and not looking down

could I have some privacy?

(a boy's voice, look down

I wasn't looking at you I was looking for the Empire State Building
—say nothing   say nothing   say nothing—)
can you go away?

(no   because you are digging a hole and that fascinates boys and
          you are burying something small wrapped in paper towel I would be afraid
to waste   in a corner   by a tree   and, all around you   a dozen tiny
popsicle crosses)

do you have any pets?

(you are crying now   crying in the first true American voice I have ever heard
          and you are a boy older than me   crying, in America
Aunt Ethel can't know about you)

Listen to me pal don't cha ever get no pets they break yer heart

(and you are running   and running fascinates boys   so does crying

I wasn't talking to anybody I was looking at the Empire State Building)
my mother: "he's very creative"

I wear leather because they kill the cows anyway   so fuck off.
I use rabbit hide glue because it firms up the canvas better than water-based
     adhesives   so go fuck yourself.
I have no problem with meat stock in my food—by that point I figure it's rather
pointless to protest   fuck you.

(repeat 98 times, every day)

or

no, sir   I have never gotten an F before
          of course I want to go to university   and I've seen all the Jason movies so
I'm not going to faint   I'm just saying   no
it's wrong   no   no way
          my parents?   tell them if you like (you see, I'm very creative)

3. The Lion Queen

for Karl Lagerfield

"weeman oo vehr my furz doo nut vorree aboht *le monde* you know?
my weeman vorree aboht Beauty"
—KL

I hate it when you're right.
You and him, both so very right together   or apart
my neighbours

in your car, walking your dog   we see   over one another
in the elevator, at the market   me picking over half-ripe bananas
you (or him) fussing for hot house lettuce from France, a flat disc of cheese,
anything Spanish or red
and inside the elevator, neighbour
it is always the ankle length sable, smelling of lanolin and offices
          listen, I have my luxuries too—a fetish for silver, money blown
on perfumes and Chinese restaurants—
but that hide of yours beats all

he sees   in the 12 seconds between the first and the ninth floor   a fag
a fag who didn't make it   a fag who forgot design school is the only way out

and I continue to shave my head because it negates you (and him)
negates excess
and people will touch me—a razor fresh head makes its own friends

Liberace and the Skinhead   we know each other we know our icons we have
2 kinds of simplicity   2 kinds of sheen   2 kinds of stunted growth
2 kinds of cuts

a fur coat and a slow elevator can teach you everything about class warfare,
men who are not the marrying type, the psychological process known as
projection, what hairdressers do in bed   and hate

or

is everything all right at home?
    (it was moving   the frog)
is there anything you'd like to get off your chest?

    (taking breath, pushing breath out)

the last student I expected to see in this office

(still wet, eyes open)

well, then, if there's nothing you want to tell me maybe the school nurse
(will see   that's a nerve   prick it and it jumps
            —don't laugh, even if you're scared—   it jumps, like clockwork)

from THE MULLIN TRILOGY

The Measure of the City not Built by Time

(prologue)

because it can burn, this place was once something like me
   organic   because it cracks (anything can)   a little bit
kept safe in the close of my palm   safe in the warm funnel of fingers
reverses spells, hands over power

but this place keeps secrets
dampens matches (thinking ahead)   values delicacy
as a bored cat prizes curious movements   with its teeth

because a City must resound (even squeak   a little bit)
let it press arabesques, curlicues   from the cut, the furrow and rise
of my ears   and dangle the casts like shells on leather strings
   —(half) circle charms to chase out devils
  then, when my ears itch   I'll know
        my name is being tossed around

1.

Christ, Andrew, this is no place
to die   so competently
wiped up after by married day nurses and a generation of charity fags
—looking through your thinning skin   into their smarter, cleaner future
          daring to call themselves angels—

Andrew   remember the plane of my floor, the spans of plank
     the broken square of my apartment

          remember the ambered wax   cross-hatched by the blacks
of table legs, grit of winter boots, chairs not lifted before left
remember yourself, better at seduction   so patient, willing to make
dumbing circles of words   over   the new kitten's trustless face
                         the colour of Angela's shoes, the time of night
          over   nothing
over   my head   and, later
(sotto vox)
          down

Angela still has those shoes. The cat will outlive you.
Andrew, this is no place to die.
          No place to make your end meet so mean a Grace—
     your life broken like table bread   jealously given
entrée   only after the better part of the meal   is gone   savoured
along the outer ring of the plate
                         (one step from the washcloth)

Andrew, the City loathes you, fishes you for compliments
wants to hear from you
     after you've gone   to tell itself how good it was to have you

die, no   this is no place to die.

2. choosing dark

you hold the day back with both hands and heavy curtains   (lowering)
     the risk, the everyday harm from sunlight
you've seen every day—(half) a lifetime—above your head, hung high
     like a warning flare   this lamp
                              casts a magic circle
          gives you enough definition
to read, change channels, take a pill, pass away

     ... from the sun outside
there's heat and violence and worse yet   time
     the path of waking hours traced   (sunspots?)
          on your skin.

3. contracting patience

cum see/cum saw
      and leapt at the chance—too good to pass up—
            and into you   it worked so many tricks, feats
(hardly) death-defying   (more like gravity, invisible to every   body
and easy to forget)

... his smile   an anxious moment before
his chin blunted his face   before you ever knew his name, his cares
or ticks   his charges

      forward, aggressive   your legs bunked square   you watched
saw a way down   stopped to pass a hand under the little freshet
called Disquiet   drinking from its mouth, found at the junction
between his heart and his eyes

      look up to the ceiling   unbuckled,
a night's tension   lets go
      at the knees and   (skip a beat) all over
      your fingers   tap boastful telegrams
            on his jawbone, under his wet chin—a chucking,
      a pat on the head—
      for your quick capture   and release.

4. getting there is half

        the alternative, the rest   is, well
The Rest   and a waiting room is any place I sit, stoop
to lace shoes   glower at crosswords ...

Oh, I can play a mean game of Hearts (have done, have done ...) or
        Badger-Your-Neighbour (with it, God's sake have done ...)
hold my own (water, shit, food)   in the coarsest events
        taking all comers—priests and doctors
going rounds   sometimes five, ten times a day

        but it's the jabs, the needlings
(between fire and chill and flame   between sheets)
        the silver and plastic prick-pockets   that get under my skin
with the best intentions

they'll trickle and prime me
(un)to death.

5. telling signs

are stairwells   they see me coming, add extra links   like tapeworms;

are old relations
gone to seed for slower reasons;

are handshakes too quick for sweat to pass between, fingerless hugs
conscious of pressure   kisses on the topmost of my cheekbone
                    the farthest point North from my smile
          from your mouth;

make this stage   this hammy denouement
plod like a Beckett play
all long breaths and blindness   piled on quarter hours of quiet prayer
fraught with stupid tension;

turn
my rumbling, jimmied tears
          into played up opening notes, chords   blown   apart;

prompt   falsettoed sobs
          as merciless as operas.

6. the measure of a city

because tongues curl the word *Justice*   in a hundred languages
I hear   only the back end of my name, spoken as a curse

because, once, I watched a tired, brown woman smooth spices
over the raked gravel   between the street and her door
         child in hand, its fingers pink with sugars

I know   my footsteps mark the city less than my blunt white face

because a single voice   (mine or yours)
can smudge the air   like an oily finger on polished brass

I understand suddenly   how to hear myself think

7. sepia

is a misunderstood colour

the earth on pink on skintan is not
the flourish of Memory   History's flare   the paint of forgetting   no

sepia is the distillation of sand, the frozen brown of March earth
the ring   retreating from a hard drop of blood long dried   it is

a colour of containment, the hue of cork cut scale thin
to shape outrageous Chinese landscapes sealed in black lacquer and glass

sepia is not the crayon cinematography of nostalgia   no
it is   the shadow over white skin in summer
in the groin of biceps   it is

the first choice of children drawing dinosaurs   it is like bricks
except it moves

I write of undefinable colours   of definition, light and clouds
a shutter snap of pigments only half-closed eyelids catch   I describe
sienna browns we know from dirty corners, the bottoms of cups
the flats of our feet
everyday smirks of colour we dismiss, scrub off   poor cousins

to the vivids   marks
we treat with bleach, rough towels   and perfumes

as we do the recent dead

(coda)

how do I measure a city not built by time?
not by the singing of boots on gridded streets
not in stately 4/4 beats
not by sound, no
Lord,   not by everything I hear

tell me, Lord   if earshot
minus   the distance from my eyes to the lamplight
times
the weight   of my body in winter clothes
is a start?

DAVID TRINIDAD

THE BOY

Looking back,
I think that he must have been an angel.
We never spoke,
but one entire summer, every day,
he sat on the curb across the street.
I watched him: thin, his skin white,
his blond hair cut short.
Sometimes, right after swimming,
his bathing suit wet and tight,
he would sit and dry off in the sun.
I couldn't stop staring.

Then late one night,
toward the end of the summer,
he appeared in my room.
Perhaps that's why
I've always considered him
an angel: silent, innocent, pale
even in the dark.
He undressed
and pulled back the sheet,
slid next to me.
His fingers felt for my lips.

But perhaps I am not remembering
correctly.
Perhaps he never came
into my room that night.
Perhaps he never existed
and I invented him.
Or perhaps it was me, not blond
but dark, who sat all summer
on that sunny corner: seventeen
and struggling to outlast
my own restlessness.

NIGHT AND FOG

(San Francisco)

Once, depressed and drunk on the worst wine, Christopher N. and I sat out on the fire escape. That was before he got weird, before I moved back to L.A.: we shared a second-floor single apartment in the Tenderloin. Christopher N. (an alias): seventeen, innocent-looking, runaway from the complacent suburbs across the bay, smiling defiler of the scriptures of his strict father, a Baptist minister. That night on the fire escape: genesis of intense gestalt friendship. Ritual of confession. We hugged each other and cried. That night I told him someday I'd write about us sitting on the fire escape. Somewhere a phone was ringing. He finished the last glass of Ripple (Pagan Pink) and pitched it at the brick wall of the opposite building. It shattered and we laughed.

Later, back inside: steam heat, *Discreet Music*, stamping on cockroaches on red carpet cigarette scars. The walls cracked like in *Repulsion*. Lavender and green lanterned light bulb of Blanche DuBois. Initiation rite: I gave him my junior high school St. Christopher (with a surfer on the other side).

Things he did I thought delightful: took taxis, wore suspenders, spit on silver cars, drew dark circles around his eyes with shoe polish for poetic effect, cut pictures out of library books and taped them to the apartment walls, insisted upon passion, allowed himself spontaneous spasms of unlimited excess, praised Tim Curry, praised Bryan Ferry, praised the gospel according to Pasolini, named his cat Icarus, created his own art form (shock), hocked records he tired of listening to to buy used books which he read and then hocked to buy our booze, spray-painted *D* in front of *ADA ST*, cried when I told him he was my Holly Golightly, cursed money for its ability to corrupt purity.

But then he got weird. St. Christopher of the Club Baths. St. Christopher of the trench coat and collect calls. His Philip Marlowe hat. St. Christopher of the transfer ticket. Turned eighteen. Moved into a condemned flat below Market. Folsom: factories murmuring all night, leather bars. St. Christopher of the post-fascist lost degeneration. Devout disciple of Peter Berlin. St. Christopher of the punk rock safety pin. Pierced his nipples. Placed explicit *Advocate* ad. St. Christopher of the forbidden fetish. The decidedly strange attraction to rubber. St. Christopher of the cock ring and handcuffs. Spiked dildo. Branded asses. Undressing in the balcony of the Strand during *Maitresse*. Blond boy snorting Rush stroking himself underneath smooth leather sucked off behind bushes in Lafayette Park after dark. St. Christopher with super-clap. St. Christopher of the 120 days of the Baptist apocalypse. Sexual dementor. Collector of dentures and dead rats, bloodletters. St. Christopher of the Castro hard hat and jockstrap. St. Christopher kicking pigeons and poodles in Union Square. St. Christopher picked up on Polk and Pine: twenty-five dollars for shitting on his trick.

My last visit to San Francisco: saw vomit on the sidewalks, saw piss streaming down steep streets. Bandaged panhandler. Black kid lifting the crutches of a fallen drunkard. Transvestite prostitute throwing beer bottles at a passing bus. Old women with shopping bag suitcases picking in trash bins as if testing produce. At the airport terminal, before he turned to go, Christopher N. said: "You're so prissy I can't see how we could ever have been friends." I flew home. *Angels of the complacent suburbs! of discotheques! of hostile police!* Got drunk.

Jeannette MacDonald, there's a dark alley for every perversion in your sickening city (water sports, B & D, fist fucking). No one is ever innocent.

TIM'S STOLEN SWEATER

Sunlight which seeps through a part
in the drapes illuminates the rumpled
contents of your suitcase: sweaters
and slacks, and some of those short-
sleeved alligator shirts, the kind
that "clones" wear, though they'd make
you look good—healthy and athletic—
unlike most of the men at the crowded
bar where we met. Before we spoke,
I wanted to reach across and touch
your cheekbone, the scar just under
the left one (I couldn't bring myself
to ask how you'd gotten it, so I
imagined a gang fight in your youth
or a steak knife in the hand of
a lover insane with jealousy). You
introduced yourself. I extended my
hand. Then, in your room, our chit-
chat continued until, abruptly, you
asked, "Do you want to kiss me?" It

was a perfect way to get to the point
and I was impressed. "Yes." Our move-
ments cast shadows of flesh barely
lit by the glow of the motel's neon
sign as it flashed on and off. Just
a few hours sleep. Now, slightly hung
over, I erase one or two of the creases
our bodies made in sheets a maid will
change later in the day, after we've
showered and dressed, gone our sep-
arate ways. You're going out for a
newspaper and a six-pack. I watch you
rummage through your suitcase, pull
on a pair of boxer shorts, jeans, and
the sweater you wore last night—
light blue with thin white stripes
around the chest—which is what I
noticed first, from across the bar,
and then, as I moved closer, how
handsome you were, despite your scar.

"C'EST PLUS QU'UN CRIME, C'EST UNE FAUTE"

for Amy Gerstler

In the small hours, several rounds
at Le Café, "one of the swankier
spots West L.A.'s nightlife offers":
pink neon and napkins, essence of
scampi and chateaubriand. Seated at
a table against the wall, listen-
ing to the couples on either side
of us chat *en français*, I was
about to comment on the "ambiance"
of the place when, struck by
the looks of a certain redheaded
waiter, you inadvertently spilled
your second strawberry daiquiri.
It seemed everyone turned to
stare at us and you blushed. I'm
afraid I didn't help much, the way
I laughed. I meant to tell you
then, but in the confusion for-
got, how last week, at work, I
found myself attracted to a rather
brawny refrigerator repairman.
He wore a tight white T-shirt,
the tattoo of a chimera half-
visible beneath one of its sleeves.

A chimera is an imaginary monster
made up of incongruous parts. It
is also a frightful or foolish
fancy. I wrote my telephone number
on a small piece of paper and
slipped it in his pocket before
he left. *Why had she acted so
very rashly?* I read this that
night at a drugstore, on the back
cover of a Harlequin Romance, as
I waited in line to buy a pack
of cigarettes. Walking home,
Hollywood Blvd. was abuzz with
tourists and various low-life
types. I reached my street. It
was late, but fireworks were still
being set off from the magicians'
private club at the top of the
hill. I stopped and looked up,
then started to laugh (It had
to be for my benefit!) as half
the night sky briefly flared
into a brilliant shade of red.

MONDAY, MONDAY

Radio's reality when
the hits just keep
happening: "I want
to kiss like lovers
do..." Why is it
I've always mistaken
these lyrics for my
true feelings? The
disc jockey says it's
spring and instantly
I'm filled with such
joy! Is it possible
that I'm experiencing
nature for the first
time? In the morning
the sun wakes me
and I am genuinely
moved, almost happy
to be alive. For a
couple of weeks it'd
been getting a little
bit brighter every
day. I wasn't aware
of this change until
the morning I noticed
the angle at which
the light hit your
GQ calendar, fully
accentuating the aus-
tere features of this
month's male model, as
I sat in the kitchen,

in your maroon robe,
and waited for my tea
to cool. I was thinking
about my feelings, about
how much I loved the sun
when I was a child and
how I loved the dark
as well, how thrilling
it was to lie in bed
on windy nights and
listen to the sound of
bushes and branches being
thrashed about outside.

Actually, that's what
I was thinking while
you were making the tea.
I was staring at the
calendar, at the smoke
from the tip of my
cigarette as it drifted
in the sunlight toward
the open window, when
you set the steaming
fifties-style cup in
front of me. Was it
at this point that
my manner changed?
Your gesture reminded
me of innumerable
mornings spent with
my parents in the pink
kitchen of my childhood.
I remembered my mother,
how she always wore her

gaudy floral bathrobe
and shuffled about in
her bedroom slippers as
she dutifully served us
breakfast. My father
sat alone at one end
of the table, his stern
face all but hidden
behind the front page
of the *Los Angeles Times*.
They seldom spoke. I
felt the tension between
them, watched with sleep-
filled eyes as he gave
her the obligatory kiss
on the cheek, then
clicked his briefcase
shut and, without a word,
walked out the door.

As I was getting dressed,
you grabbed me, kissed
me on the lips, said
something romantic.
I left your apartment
feeling confused, got
on the freeway and
inched my way through
the bumper-to-bumper
traffic. I was confused
about sex, about the
unexpected ambivalence
which, the night before,
prompted my hesitancy
and nonchalant attitude:
"It's late," I said,
"Let's just sleep."
The cars ahead of me
wouldn't budge. I
turned on the radio and
started changing stations.
I was afraid I would
always be that anxious,
that self-obsessed, that
I might never be able
to handle a mature
relationship. Stuck on
the freeway like that,
I was tempted to get
into it, the pain and
the drama, but the mood
soon passed. (After
all, it *is* spring.)
At last, traffic picked
up and I enjoyed the
rest of the drive, kept
the radio on all
the way to work and
listened to all those
songs, though I finally
realized those songs
were no longer my feelings.

MEET THE SUPREMES

When Petula Clark sang "Downtown," I wished I
could go there with her. I wanted to be free
to have fun and fall in love, but from suburbia
the city appeared more distant and dangerous
than it actually was. I withdrew and stayed
in my room, listened to Jackie DeShannon sing
"What The World Needs Now Is Love." I agreed,
but being somewhat morose considered the song
a hopeless plea. I listened to Skeeter Davis'
"The End Of The World" and decided that was
what it would be when I broke up with my first
boyfriend. My head spun as fast as the singles
I saved pennies to buy: "It's My Party," "Give
Him A Great Big Kiss," "(I Want To Be) Bobby's
Girl," "My Guy"—the list goes on. At the age
of ten, I rushed to the record store to get
"Little" Peggy March's smash hit, "I Will Follow
Him." An extreme example of lovesick devotion,
it held down the top spot on the charts for
several weeks in the spring of 1963. "Chapel
Of Love" came out the following year and was
my favorite song for a long time. The girls
who recorded it, The Dixie Cups, originally
called themselves Little Miss & The Muffets.
They cut three hits in quick succession, then
disappeared. I remember almost the exact moment
I heard "Johnny Angel" for the first time: it
came on the car radio while we were driving
down to Laguna Beach to visit some friends of
the family. In the back seat, I set the book I'd
been reading beside me and listened, completely
mesmerized by Shelley Fabares' dreamy, teenage
desire. Her sentimental lyrics continue to move
me (although not as intensely) to this day.
Throughout adolescence, no other song affected
        me quite like that one.
On my transistor, I listened to the Top Twenty

countdown as, week after week, more girl singers
and groups
came and went than I could keep track of:

Darlene Love,
Brenda Lee,
Dee Dee Sharp,
Martha Reeves
& The Vandellas,
The Chantels,
The Shirelles,
The Marvelettes,
The Ronettes,
The Girlfriends,
The Rag Dolls,
The Cinderellas,
Alice Wonderland,
Annette, The
Beach-Nuts, Nancy
Sinatra, Little
Eva, Veronica,
The Pandoras,
Bonnie & The
Treasures,
The Murmaids,
Evie Sands,
The Pussycats,
The Patty Cakes,
The Tran-Sisters,
The Pixies Three,
The Toys, The
Juliettes and
The Pirouettes,
The Charmettes,
The Powder Puffs,

Patti Lace &
The Petticoats,
The Rev-Lons,
The Ribbons,
The Fashions,
The Petites,
The Pin-Ups,
Cupcakes,
Chic-Lets,
Jelly Beans,
Cookies, Goodies,
Sherrys, Crystals,
Butterflys,
Bouquets,
Blue-Belles,
Honey Bees,
Dusty Springfield,
The Raindrops,
The Blossoms,
The Petals,
The Angels,
The Halos,
The Hearts,
The Flamettes,
The Goodnight
Kisses, The
Strangeloves,
and The Bitter
Sweets.

I was ecstatic when "He's So Fine" hit the #1 spot.
I couldn't get the lyrics out of my mind and continued
to hum "Doo-lang Doo-lang Doo-lang" long after

puberty ended, a kind of secret anthem. Although
The Chiffons tried to repeat their early success
with numerous singles, none did as well as their
first release. "Sweet Talkin' Guy" came close,
sweeping them back into the Top Ten for a short
time, but after that there were no more hits.
Lulu made her mark in the mid-sixties with "To Sir
    With Love,"
which I would put on in order to daydream about
my junior high algebra instructor. By then I was
a genuine introvert. I'd come home from school,
having been made fun of for carrying my textbooks
like a girl, and listen to song after song from
my ever-expanding record collection. In those
days, no one sounded sadder than The Shangri-Las.
Two pairs of sisters from Queens, they became famous
for their classic "death disc shocker," "Leader Of
    The Pack,"
and for their mod look. They were imitated (but
    never equalled)
by such groups as The Nu-Luvs and The Whyte Boots.
The Shangri-Las stayed on top for a couple of
years, then lost their foothold and split up.
Much later, they appeared in rock 'n' roll revival
shows, an even sadder act since Marge, the fourth
member of the band, had died of an accidental
drug overdose. I started smoking cigarettes around
this time, but wouldn't discover pills, marijuana
or alcohol until my final year of high school.
I loved Lesley Gore because she was always crying
and listened to "As Tears Go By" till the single had
so many scratches I couldn't play it anymore.
I preferred Marianne Faithfull to The Beatles and
The Rolling Stones, was fascinated by the stories
about her heroin addiction and suicide attempt.
She's still around. So is Diana Ross. She made
it to superstardom alone, maintaining the success
she'd previously achieved as the lead singer of
The Supremes, one of the most popular girl groups
of all time. Their debut album was the first LP

I owned. Most of the songs on it were hits—
one would reach the top of the charts as another
hit the bottom. Little did I know, as I listened
to "Nothing But Heartaches" and "Where Did Our Love
Go," that nearly twenty years later I would hit
bottom in an unfurnished Hollywood single, drunk
and stoned and fed up, still spinning those same
old tunes. The friction that already existed
within The Supremes escalated in 1967 as Diana
Ross made plans for her solo career. The impending
split hit Florence the hardest. Rebelliously,
she gained weight and missed several performances,
and was finally told to leave the group. The pain
she experienced in the years that followed was
a far cry from the kind of anguish expressed
in The Supremes' greatest hits. Florence lost
the lawsuit she filed against Motown, failed at
a solo career of her own, went through a bitter
divorce, and ended up on welfare. In this classic
photograph of the group, however, Florence is
smiling. Against a black backdrop, she and Mary
look up at and frame Diana, who stands in profile
and raises her right hand, as if toward the future.
The girls' sequinned and tasselled gowns sparkle
as they strike dramatic poses among some Grecian
columns. Thus, The Supremes are captured forever
like this, in an unreal, silvery light. That
moment, they're in heaven. Then, at least for Flo,
begins the long and painful process of letting go.

MOVIN' WITH NANCY

It is almost time to grow up
I eat my TV dinner and watch
Nancy Sinatra in 1966
All boots and thick blonde hair

I eat my TV dinner and watch
The daughter of Frank Sinatra
All boots and thick blonde hair
She appears on "The Ed Sullivan Show"

The daughter of Frank Sinatra
She sings "These Boots Are Made For Walkin'"
She appears on "The Ed Sullivan Show"
The song becomes a number one hit

She sings "These Boots Are Made For Walkin'"
She sings "Somethin' Stupid" with her father
The song becomes a number one hit
She marries and divorces singer/actor Tommy Sands

She sings "Somethin' Stupid" with her father
She sings "The Last Of The Secret Agents"
She marries and divorces singer/actor Tommy Sands
She sings "How Does That Grab You, Darlin'?"

She sings "The Last Of The Secret Agents"
She sings "Lightning's Girl" and "Friday's Child"
She sings "How Does That Grab You, Darlin'?"
She sings "Love Eyes" and "Sugar Town"

She sings "Lightning's Girl" and "Friday's Child"
She puts herself in the hands of writer/producer Lee Hazelwood
She sings "Love Eyes" and "Sugar Town"
She co-stars with Elvis Presley in *Speedway*

She puts herself in the hands of writer/producer Lee Hazelwood
Three gold records later
She co-stars with Elvis Presley in *Speedway*
She rides on Peter Fonda's motorcycle

Three gold records later
She has developed an identity of her own
She rides on Peter Fonda's motorcycle
The wild angels roar into town

She has developed an identity of her own
Nancy Sinatra in 1966
The wild angels roar into town
It is almost time to grow up

HAND OVER HEART

I look up at the clock.
It's time to go, so
I cover the typewriter
and calculator, lock my radio
in the file cabinet
and straighten my desk.
On the way out, I unplug
the Christmas tree lights.
I am rarely the last one
to leave the office.

Alone in the elevator,
I listen to a lilting
rendition of "Frosty
The Snowman." The door
slides open. Outside,
it's already dark. I say
good night to the guard
in the parking lot, wait
for my car to warm up.
It does and I drive off.

Halfway home,
I turn on the radio.
Madonna sings
her new hit, "Open
Your Heart." At
the same time, on
another station,
Cyndi Lauper sings
her latest song, "Change
Of Heart." Not that long
ago, it might have
been Brenda Lee
singing "Heart In Hand"
and Connie Francis
belting out any number
of her most popular

tunes: "My Heart
Has A Mind Of Its
Own," "Breakin' In
A Brand New Broken
Heart," "When
The Boy In Your Arms
(Is The Boy In Your
Heart)" or "Don't
Break The Heart
That Loves You."
I don't know why
I think about
such things.

I park the car
in the garage, walk
across the courtyard
and check the mailbox.
A few bills, ads,
Christmas cards
from friends I no
longer feel that
close to. No
messages on my
phone machine.

"I'm sorry,"
you said last
night. You seemed
sincere. Later,
I sat in my car
and cried. *Was it
love? I thought
it was love. I mean
it felt like love.*
It really did.

DRIVING BACK FROM NEW HAVEN

Tim looks at his watch, reaches into his
pocket, takes out a small plastic container
and swallows an AZT pill with a sip of Sprite.
"Poison," he mutters under his breath. I
glance over at him. We haven't talked about
his health the entire trip. "How does it
make you feel?" I ask. "Like I want to live
until they discover a cure," he snaps. We
travel in silence for a while. I stare out
the window at all the green trees on the
Merritt Parkway. Then he says: "I resent
it. I resent that we were not raised with
an acceptance of death. And here it is,
all around us. And I fucking resent it.
I resent that we do not know how to die."

SUNDAY EVENING

Back from Boston,
Ira and I listen
to a tape of Anne Sexton
reading her poems—
part of my $87.00 binge
at the Grolier Book Shop
in Harvard Square.
Ira likes her "smoky" voice,
which is interrupted
by the kettle's shrill whistle.
I go into the kitchen
and prepare our tea:
Cranberry Cove for Ira,
Mellow Mint for me.
We sip, smoke and listen
to Anne. Toward the end
of the tape, Ira unpacks
the little black bag
of Godiva chocolates
and, one by one, eats
a butterscotch-filled coat
of arms, a light brown starfish
and a gold-foiled cherry cordial.
He chews and smiles.
I regret that I ate all
of mine on the train.
But wait! He offers me
his last one (which he
makes me earn with kisses):
a dark chocolate heart.

PEE SHY

I waited till
the boys' room
was empty, then
stood at one
of the urinals.
It always took
me a long
time, even when
I was alone.
Before I could
do it, someone
came in and
stood next to
me. Anxiously, I
glanced over. It
was Steve, the
good-looking son
of an actor
on a popular
detective series. He
was one grade
ahead of me.
Everyone said he
was stuck-up,
but I'd always
had a crush
on him. As
we stood beside
each other, my
legs began to
shake. I tried
to look straight
at the wall
in front of
me. Without realizing
it, however, I
pressed my whole

body against the
urinal. "Don't worry,"
Steve said disdainfully,
"I'm not looking
at you." He
pulled the handle
above his urinal,
zipped up his
pants. Out of
the corner of
my eye, I
watched him wash
his hands and
check his hair
in the mirror.
Then he left.

I can't remember
anything after that.
How long did
I stand there?
Did I rush
to my locker?
Was I late
for a period
I dreaded—woodshop,
drafting, gym? How
did I hide
my shame, convinced
as I was—
as I'm sure
I was—that
everyone would know
my hideous secret
before I even reached
my next class?

FAMILY PORTRAIT, 1963

My father sits in his dark
armchair, under a store-bought
painting of Paris,
reading *Fortune* magazine.
As a young man
he read Shakespeare and Poe,
dreamed of being an artist
(my mother tells me this).
Now he works somewhere
every day, and at night
barks orders: *Sit up
straight! Get out
of my sight! Stop
that racket! Goddamnit!
Turn down the TV!*

★

My mother sobs
behind her locked bedroom door:
*Your father's a tyrant.
Go away.* Other nights
she has migraines
and lies in agony

on the living room couch
while my father yells
Get up, you fat slob!
Do some work around here!
I do chores for her, sneak
her cigarettes and chocolate bars
into the house, hide them
in the pots and pans.
When they fight, I lock
myself in the pink bathroom,
play with the soap roses
in the shell-shaped dish,
with her delicate perfume bottles
and her Avon lipsticks—
so many names for red.

★

My brother collects
baseball cards,
                for my father

builds model airplanes
and race cars,
                for my father

watches *Gunsmoke*
and *Combat,*
                for my father

joins Boy Scouts
and Little League,
                for my father

mows the lawn,
pulls the weeds,
rakes the leaves,
            for my father

excels in batting
and tackling
and running,
            for my father

and brings home
poor grades on
his report card.

And is punished
by my father.

                ★

One of my sisters stands
at a miniature bassinet
changing the diaper
on her Hush-a-Bye Baby.
(Someday she'll have four
children of her own, bounced
checks, bruises and black eyes,
a husband she'll try, repeatedly,
to leave.) With a makebelieve
iron, she unwrinkles the doll's
frilly pink party frock.
She's my father's favorite:
the quietest one.

＊

My other sister learns
to walk early, is always
breaking things. One night,
when my father barks an order
at the dinner table, she puts her
little hands on her hips
and barks back: *You're
not the boss! I am!*
After a tense silence,
my father's face seems to
crack, and he laughs.
Then we all laugh.

＊

At school, I spend
most of the lunch hour
in the library.
I belong to
the Bookworm Club:
the more I read,
the higher my name moves up
the bespectacled paper worm
on the bulletin board.
I'm reading the *Little House*
series and the blue biographies
of famous Americans,
but only the women:
Pocahontas, Martha Washington,
Betsy Ross.

In the afternoon,
I do homework
at the kitchen table
while my mother cooks and cleans.
I ask her questions,
but there's a lot she doesn't know.
She hands me a warm Toll House cookie,
tells me to look for the answer
in the book.

Around 4:30, she sprays
lilac-scented Glade
to cover up the smell
of her cigarettes.
When my father's car
pulls in the driveway,
she franticly sets out
napkins, glasses, handfuls
of silverware.
Make yourself scarce.
I gather my books and papers
together, rush down the hall
to my bedroom, hear
the door slam.

PLAYING WITH DOLLS

Every weekend morning, I'd sneak downstairs to play
with my sisters' Barbie dolls. They had all
of them: Barbie, Ken, Allan, Midge, Skipper and
Skooter. They even had the little freckled boy,
Ricky ("Skipper's Friend"), and Francie, "Barbie's
'MOD'ern cousin." Quietly, I'd set the dolls

in front of their wardrobe cases, take the dolls'
clothes off miniature plastic hangers, and play
until my father woke up. There were several Barbies—
blonde ponytail, black bubble, brunette flip—all
with the same pointed tits, which (odd for a boy)
didn't interest me as much as the dresses and

accessories. I'd finger each glove and hat and
necklace and high heel, then put them on the dolls.
Then I'd invent elaborate stories. A "creative" boy,
I could entertain myself for hours. I liked to play
secretly like that, though I often got caught. All
my father's tirades ("Boys don't play with Barbies!

It isn't *normal!*") faded as I slipped Barbie's
perfect figure into her stunning ice blue and
sea green satin and tulle formal gown. All
her outfits had names like "Fab Fashion," "Doll's
Dream" and "Golden Evening"; Ken's were called "Play
Ball!," "Tennis Pro," "Campus Hero" and "Fountain Boy,"

which came with two tiny sodas and spoons. Model boy
that he was, Ken hunted, fished, hit home runs. Barbie's
world revolved around garden parties, dances, play
and movie dates. A girl with bracelets and scarves and
sunglasses and fur stoles.... "Boys don't play with dolls!"
My parents were arguing in the living room. "All

boys do." As always, my mother defended me. "All
sissies!" snarled my father. "He's a creative boy,"
my mother responded. I stuffed all the dresses and dolls
and shoes back into the black cases that said "Barbie's
Wonderful World" in swirling pink letters and
clasped them shut. My sisters, awake now, wanted to play

with me. "I can't play," I said, "Dad's upset." All
day, he stayed upset. Finally, my mother came upstairs
    and said, "You're a boy,
David. Forget about Barbies. Stop playing with dolls."

ANSWER SONG

for Tim Dlugos

Lesley Gore got her rival good
in the smash answer to "It's My Party,"
"Judy's Turn To Cry," when her
unfaithful boyfriend, Johnny, suddenly
came to his senses in the midst
of yet another apparently unchaperoned shindig.
I picture Judy—hot pink mini-dress
and ratted black hair—being swept away
by a flood of her own teenage tears.
In triumph, Lesley rehangs Johnny's ring
around her neck. She has no idea that
the British are coming, that her popularity
will wane and she'll watch her hits drop
off the charts like so many tinkling
heart-shaped charms, and that there she'll be:
a has-been at seventeen. Naturally
she'll finish high school and marry
Johnny. They'll have a couple of kids
and settle down in a yellow two-story
tract house with white-shuttered windows
and bright red flower beds. At the supermart,
Lesley will fill her cart with frozen dinners,
which she'll serve with a smile as the family
gathers round their first color TV.

Week after week, she'll exchange recipes,
attend PTA meetings and Tupperware parties,
usher Brownie troops past tar pits
and towering dinosaur bones. Whenever
she hears one of her songs on an oldie station,
she'll think about those extinct beasts.
She'll think about them too as, year
after year, she tosses headlines
into the trash: Vietnam, Nixon, Patty Hearst.
Then one afternoon—her children grown
and gone—she'll discover a strange
pair of earrings in the breast pocket
of Johnny's business suit. It's downhill
after that: curlers, migraines, fattening
midnight snacks. Or is it? She did,
after all, sing "You Don't Own Me,"
the first pop song with a feminist twist.
What if Lesley hears about women's lib?
What if she goes into therapy and begins
to question her attraction to emotionally
unavailable men? Suppose, under hypnosis,
she returns to her sixteenth birthday party,
relives all those tears, and learns that
it was Judy—not Johnny—she'd wanted
all along. There's no answer to that
song, of course, but I have
heard rumors.

THE TEN BEST EPISODES OF *THE PATTY DUKE SHOW*

1. Patty cheats on a computerized intelligence test and is pronounced a genius.

2. Ross blackmails Patty and Cathy by tape recording their conversation at a slumber party.

3. Patty is cast as Cleopatra in the school play, but gets stage fright on opening night.

4. Patty writes a novel entitled *I Was a Teenage Teenager.*

5. Cathy wears Patty's expensive new dress to a piano concert and accidentally spills punch on it.

6. Patty and Cathy run against each other for class president.

7. Frankie Avalon's car breaks down in front of the Lane house.

8. Patty raffles a date with Richard for the church bazaar, then gets jealous and tries to buy all the tickets back.

9. Patty's tonsils are taken out by a dreamboat doctor (played by Troy Donahue).

10. Patty pretends to be Cathy and flirts with Richard to see if he'll be faithful to her.

THINGS TO DO IN
VALLEY OF THE DOLLS (The Movie)

Move to New York.
Lose your virginity.
Become a star.
Send money to your mother.

Call pills "dolls."
Fire the talented newcomer.
Have a nervous breakdown.
Suffer from an incurable degenerative disease.

Sing the theme song.
Do your first nude scene.
Wear gowns designed by Travilla.
Become addicted to booze and dope.

Scream "Who needs you!"
Stagger around in a half-slip and bra.
Come to in a sleazy hotel room.
Say "I am merely traveling incognito."

Get drummed out of Hollywood.
Come crawling back to Broadway.
Pull off Susan Hayward's wig
and try to flush it down the toilet.

End up in a sanitarium.
Hiss "It wasn't a nuthouse!"
Get an abortion.
Go on a binge.

Detect a lump in your breast.
Commit suicide.
Make a comeback.
Overact.

ACCESSORIES

for Beauregard Houston-Montgomery

Vinyl fashion doll
comes with swimsuit, pearl earrings,
sunglasses and shoes.

★

Pastel slip, panties
and strapless bra come with comb,
brush and "real" mirror.

★

Baby dolls come with
"Dear Diary," brass alarm
clock and wax apple.

(Note: Ken's pajamas
come with same clock, glass of milk
and wax sugar bun.)

★

Sheer negligee comes
with pink pompon scuffs and stuffed
dog for Barbie's bed.

★

Robe comes with shower
cap, soap, "Hers" towel, powder
puff and box of talc.

(Note: Ken's robe comes with
white briefs, "His" towel, sponge and
electric razor.)

★

Sunback dress comes with
chef's hat, apron, four uten-
sils and potholder.

★

Blue jumper comes with
black plastic serving tray and
two soft drinks and straws.

(Note: straws are extreme-
ly difficult for Barbie
collectors to find.)

★

Turtleneck and skirt
come with scissors, needles, yarns
and "How to Knit" book.

★

Cotton dress comes with
cartwheel hat, necklace, tele-
phone and fruit-filled tote.

★

Nurse set comes with spec-
tacles, hot water bottle,
cough syrup and spoon.

(Note: "Dr. Ken" comes
with surgeon's mask, medical
bag and stethoscope.)

★

Checked shirt and jeans come
with wedgies, picnic basket,
fish and bamboo pole.

★

Brocade dress and coat
come with corduroy clutch, fur
hat, gloves and hankie.

★

Pink satin formal
comes with mink stole, pearl choker
and clear glittered pumps.

★

Leotard, tutu
and tights come with pink shoe bag
for ballet slippers.

★

Waltz-length party dress
comes with petticoat, picture
hat and sequined purse.

★

Sleek nightclub gown comes
with black gloves, bead necklace, mi-
crophone and pink scarf.

★

Wedding dress comes with
veil, graduated pearls, blue
garter and bouquet.

(Note: ring, on tiny
satin pillow, comes only
with deluxe Wedding

Party Gift Set, which
includes Barbie in "Bride's Dream,"
Ken in "Tuxedo,"

Midge in "Orange Blos-
som" and Skipper in "Flower
Girl." Mint-in-box set

is scarce and consid-
ered quite a gold mine on the
collector's market.)

FLUFF

for Lynn Crosbie

O Fluff, no one knows who you are.
You were produced for one brief year
(nineteen seventy-one) after
Mattel discontinued Skooter,
Barbie's little sister Skipper's
best friend. The toy company feared
the first generation of Bar-
bie consumers, baby boomers
nearing their teens, would disappear
once puberty struck. So you were
invented, a fresh face to lure
the next wave of greedy youngsters,
pink pocketbooks full of gener-
ous allowances or hard-earned
baby-sitting money, to stores
with well-stocked doll departments, where
you were displayed, a wide-eyed, cheer-
ful, puffy-cheeked tomboy, blonde hair
in twin ponytails, wearing your
green, yellow and orange striped over-
alls. You came with a skateboard, per-
fect for cruisin' the park after
school with your pal, Growing Up Skipper.
Mattel executives were sure
that you would be a best-seller,

but your short shelf life was over
almost as soon as it had start-
ed. In essence, Fluff, you flopped. More-
over, today, when collectors
are willing to pay ten dollars
for a pair of Barbie shoes, you're
not worth a lot, even NRFB (Never
Removed From Box). I remember
you, though. As a child, I smeared your
cheeks with grease and slid you under
my girlfriend's orange plastic camper.
Barbie dolls were far too mature
for a girl like me to endure.
But not your flat-chested allure!
O tiny mechanic! The cars
I made you tune up and repair!
The engines you put together!
The windshields you washed, the batter-
ies you changed, tires you filled with air!
After work, you'd smoke a cigar-
ette, then skateboard home in the dark.
O smudged kid! O angry loner!
All my friends think that I'm bizarre
'cause Fluff, no one knows who you are.

THE GAME OF LIFE

I start with $2,000 and a car.
Click, click, click...
spin the Wheel of Fate and

eagerly advance.
At the first fork in the road, I
decide to take

the longer way through college
with a chance
for a larger salary. *Click, click, click.*

Lawyer! (Salary $15,000)
Move ahead four spaces. PAY DAY!
On the first mountain

range, I find a uranium deposit
and collect $100,000.
At the church I stop and get

married: add
spouse, collect presents and go
on honeymoon

(five spaces). *Click, click, click.*
Many surprises
are in store for me on Life's

winding road:
win $50,000 at the race track
and triple it by

betting on the wheel; add a baby
daughter (pink peg)
then twin sons (two blue pegs);

become a sweep-
stakes winner; even take revenge
on my opponent

(sending him back ten spaces).
After I cross
the third mountain range, I

incur some
major expenses: buy a helicopter
($40,000); take

world cruise ($8,000); expand
business ($50,000);
pay $9,000 to get rid of uncle's

skunk farm.
But I keep passing PAY DAY!
and collecting

dividends on my stock. Stop
to fish on
Toll Bridge: lose turn. Cyclone

wrecks home!
(I'm insured.) Pay $5,000 for tou-
pee. The Day of

Reckoning is a breeze—no Poor
Farm for me!
I receive $20,000 for each child

and proceed.
Click, click, click. Buy phony
diamond from

best friend. Pay $10,000. This,
just one space
before Millionaire Acres!

DIRECTIONS

First, disconnect
smoke detectors
and dim all lights.
If desired: soft

music, incense.
Take the letters
of an ex-friend
(ten years worth) and

place them in your
kitchen sink. Douse
thoroughly with
lighter fluid

and ignite. Add
postcards, photo-
graphs, poems, notes—
any items

you might have cher-
ished as much as
you cherished said
so-called friend. Fan

the flames; let their
heat redden your
cheeks. Breathe in the
black smoke. Hold it.

Exhale. Begin
to feel unbur-
dened, free. Laugh out
loud: you've destroyed

a little piece
of that person's
voice. Scoop ashes
into plastic

trash bag. Top with
eggshells, coffee
grounds. Spit. Repeat
as needed, as

others either
betray or a-
bandon you, or
just let you down.

RED PARADE

Depressed because my
book wasn't nominated
for a gay award,

I lie on the couch
watching—not listening to—
the O.J. trial.

Byron, who senses
something's wrong, hides under the
bed until Ira

comes home, carrying
a bouquet of beautifully
wrapped tulips. I press

the mute button. "*This*
is your prize," he says. "Guess what
they're called." A smile in-

voluntarily
overcomes my frown. "What?" "Red
Parade." "That sounds like

the name of an old
Barbie outfit," I say. "That's
exactly what I

told the florist. And
you know what she told me?" "What?"
"When she was a girl,

she turned her Barbie
into Cleopatra: gave
her an Egyptian

haircut and painted
her nipples blue." "How cool." "Yeah,
but now she thinks that

her doll would be worth
eight hundred dollars if she
hadn't messed it up."

Once in water, the
tulips begin to unclench—
ten angry fists. Their

colors are fierce, like
Plath's "great African cat," her
"bowl of red blooms." Poor

Sylvia, who so
desperately wanted awards,
and only won them

after she was dead.
Byron jumps up, Ira sits
down and massages

my feet. "You guys." My
spirits are lifted by their
tulips, kisses, licks.

ACKNOWLEDGEMENTS

Jeffery Conway's poems "Photo" and "Blood" appeared for the first time in *The James White Review*; "HIV" and "Tuesday Night" appeared in *Brooklyn Review*; "Hangover" was first published in *Queer City, The Portable Lower East Side*; "Sestina to a Tattooed Boy" and "Fire Island" first appeared in *B City*; "Sister" and "Fall in Tompkins Square Park" appeared in *Columbia Poetry Review*; and "To an Angel" first appreared in *Northridge Review*.

Sky Gilbert's poems "Once When I Was in a Play," "Seven Sillinesses" and "The Island of Lost Tears" have all been previously published in *The Church and Wellesley Review*.

Courtnay McFarlane's "Craig" was first published in *Fiery Spirits* (HarperCollins, 1995); "Catharsis" first appeared in *Word Up* (Key Porter Books, 1995).

David Trinidad's poems "The Boy" and "Night and Fog" first appeared in *Pavane* by David Trinidad (Sherwood Press, 1981); "Tim's Stolen Sweater," "C'est plus qu'un crime, c'est une faute," "Monday, Monday," "Meet the Supremes," "Movin' with Nancy" and "Hand Over Heart" are from *Hand Over Heart: Poems 1981-1988* (Serpent's Tail, 1991); "Driving Back from New Haven," "Sunday Evening," "Pee Shy," "Family Portrait, 1963," "Playing with Dolls," "Answer Song," "The Ten Best Episodes of *The Patty Duke Show*" and "Things to Do in *Valley of the Dolls* (The Movie)" are from *Answer Song* (High Risk/Serpent's Tail, 1994); "Accessories" first appeared in *Exact Change Yearbook*; "Fluff" originally appeared in *The Baffler*; and "The Game of Life" appeared for the first time in *Columbia Poetry Review*.

R.M. Vaughan's "10 Reasons Why I Fall in Love with Innaccessible Straight Boys Every Damn Time" appeared for the first time in *Sin Over Tan* (Toronto); "Doctors Faustus" appeared in *Expressions* (Saint Paul, MN); "A Thin Man" appeared in *Orbis* (Warwickshire, UK); "3 Poems for Paul Bowles" was first published in *The New Brunswick Reader* (Saint John); portions of "Sickness Lexicon" appeared in *The Fiddlehead* (Fredericton); and "3 Possible Titles for a Poem about Animals" first appeared in *Pan Del Muerto* (Toronto).